DATE DUE

DEMCO 38-296

The Marshall Cavendish Illustrated History of

POPULAR MUSIC

Volume 13

1974-1975

MARSHALL CAVENDISH
NEW YORK, LONDON, TORONTO, SYDNEY

Reference Edition Published 1990

...on

...a. Vicenza.

Reference edition produced by DPM Services.

© Orbis Publishing Ltd.MCMLXXXIX
© Marshall Cavendish Ltd.MCMLXXXIX

Set ISBN 1-85436-015-3

Library of Congress Cataloging in Publication Data

The Marshall Cavendish history of popular music.
    p.   cm.
    Includes index.
    ISBN 1-85435-028-5 (vol. 13)
    1. Popular music − History and criticism. 2. Rock music − History
and Criticism. I. Marshall Cavendish Corporation. II. Title:
History of popular music.
ML 3470. M36 1988
784. 5' 009 − dc19   88-21076
                                                              CIP
                                                              MN

Editorial Staff

Editor	Ashley Brown
Executive Editors	Adrian Gilbert
	Michael Heatley
Consultant Editors	Richard Williams
	Peter Brookesmith
Editorial Director	Brian Innes

Reference Edition Staff

Reference Editor	Mark Dartford
Revision Editor	Fran Jones
Consultant Editor	Michael Heatley
Art Editor	Graham Beehag

CONTENTS

CONTRIBUTORS

CLIVE ANDERSON

Co-author of *The Soul Book* and contributor to *Encyclopedia of Rock*, he has also written for *Black Music, Black Echoes, New Kommotion* and other magazines.

STEPHEN BARNARD

Has contributed to *Atlantic Rock, Melody Maker* and the *Rock Files* series. He also lectures at the City University, London.

DICK BRADLEY

Completed his PhD thesis on *British Popular Music in the Fifties* at the Centre of Contemporary Cultural Studies in Birmingham, England, and has also written articles for *Media, Culture & Society.*

JOHN BROVEN

Author of *Walking to New Orleans* and *South of Louisiana*, he has also contributed to *Nothing but the Blues* and *Encyclopedia of Rock*. He writes for *Blues Unlimited* and has also compiled several New Orleans rhythm and blues anthologies

ROB FINNIS

Author of *The Phil Spector Story* and *The Gene Vincent Story*, he has contributed to the major rock journals and runs a specialist record shop.

SIMON FRITH

A lecturer at the University of Warwick, England, he has built up a reputation over the last 15 years as one of the leading international commentators on rock music. He has co-edited the *Rock File* series, and written *The Sociology of Rock.*

PETER GURALNIK

Author of *Feel Like Going Home, Lost Highway* and *Nighthawk Blues*, his articles on blues, country and rock have appeared in *Rolling Stone*, the *Village Voice, Country Music, Living Blues*, the *New York Times* and the *Boston Phoenix.*

BILL HARRY

Founder member of UK's *Mersey Beat*, he later became news editor of *Record Mirror* and music columnist for *Weekend*. He is currently an independent PR for such artists as Suzi Quatro and Kim Wilde.

MARTIN HAWKINS

An acknowledged expert on the Sun era of rock'n'roll (author of *The Sun Story*), he writes for *Melody Maker, Time Barrier Express* and *Country Music*

BRIAN HOGG

Publisher of *Bam Balam*, which concentrates on US and UK bands of the Sixties, he has also written for such magazines as *New York Rocker* and *Record Collector.*

PETER JONES

Was editor of UK's *Record Mirror* from 1961 to 1969. He then became UK News editor of *Billboard* in 1977 and later UK and European Editor.

ROBIN KATZ

After 10 years in the Motown Press Office, she now writes freelance for *New Sound, New Styles, International Musician* and *Smash Hits.*

JOE McEWEN

An acknowledged authority on soul music, he has written for *Rolling Stone, Phonograph Record, Black Music*, the *Boston Phoenix* and Boston's *Real Paper.*

BILL MILLAR

As a freelance journalist he writes for *Melody Maker* and other rock papers. He is the author of *The Drifters* and *The Coasters.*

DAVID MORSE

Author of *Motown*, he lectures at the School of English and American Studies at Sussex University, England.

TONY RUSSELL

Editor of *Old Time Music* from 1971, he contributes regularly to *Blues Unlimited* and *Jazz Journal* and is the author of *Blacks, Whites and Blues.*

ROBERT SHELTON

Has written about blues, country and folk for the *New York Times* , London *Times, Listener, Time Out* and *Melody Maker.*

NICK TOSCHES

Author of *Hellfire*, a biography of Jerry Lee Lewis, he also writes for *New York Times* and *Village Voice.*

MICHAEL WATTS

Writes on popular arts for *The Los Angeles Times* and London *Times* and is rock columnist for *Records and Recording Magazine.*

ADAM WHITE

Has written about Motown for *Music Week* and *Black Echoes*, and scripted a six-hour documentary about the company and its music for US radio. Also worked as managing editor of *Billboard* magazine in New York.

Southern Comfort

**New directions and old favourites
from below the Mason Dixon line**

AMONG THE MANY CONFLICTS that rack the American soul and disturb the nation's delicate equilibrium, the struggle between the South and the North is probably one of the deepest-felt and most significant. It began with the very origins of modern America, in the differences between Southern plantation life and the Northern manufacturing communities, and solidified over the bloody issue of slavery. The Civil War of 1861-65 – the culmination of the South-North conflict – was the most catastrophic episode in a struggle that has helped shape America.

The conflict between North and South has never been narrowly political, much less simply geographic. It has always been more about ideas and attitudes; at one time the South was identified with agriculture-based values, the North with industry-based values. The struggle between South and North has been seen, at different times, as a struggle between conservatism and liberalism, freedom and restraint, tradition and progress, family

To many members of the liberal rock community of the late Sixties, the South stank of bigotry and oppression. Many Southern musicians resented this glib scapegoating, however, and attempted to affirm their pride in their background – though some, like Lynyrd Skynyrd (above), appeared to condone the worst aspects of Southern history.

and community, moralism and pragmatism, but what matters is the struggle itself.

Since the Second World War, the South has become an umbrella term for all the states in a broad arc from California to Virginia – the so-called Southern Rim or New South. They house the main centres of America's profitable new industries (electronics, entertainment and oil); they have provided many of the country's presidents; they beam the sun-tanned, peach-fed image of modern America across the world in the shape of country and country-based music, films like *Smokey And The Bandit* (1977) and TV shows like 'Dallas'. Rock music has reflected this upturn of the South's fortunes.

Rock King

Fifties rock'n'roll was largely a Southern music – because its components, like blues and rockabilly, were rooted in Southern experience, and because it saw itself as essentially a rebel music nurtured outside the New York music business establishment and identifying with the needs and values of the young, the poor and the angry. Rock'n'roll changed the face of contemporary culture. It elevated a poor, Southern white boy named Elvis Presley to the rank of king. Elvis was born in Tupelo, Mississippi, and recorded and spent most of his life in Memphis; Fats Domino was born and recorded in New Orleans; Gene Vincent, born in Norfolk, Virginia, recorded there and in Nashville; Buddy Holly, born in Lubbock, Texas, recorded in Clovis, New Mexico. And, although Eddie Cochran spent his childhood in Oklahoma and Minnesota, from 1949 he lived in Southern California and started his professional life as a rockabilly singer playing the American Southwest.

One important aspect of the relationship between rock'n'roll and the South is the way in which Southern-based independent record companies like Houston's Duke/Peacock, Memphis' Sun and Dot of Gallatin, Tennessee, blossomed with rock'n'roll's mass appeal. By the late Fifties, the South and Southern music – in one form or another – had become the focus of activity for a large portion of the American record industry. What had once been a minority music (whether it was country or blues-based) was, in the guise of rock'n'roll, rapidly attracting a wider audience.

Art and soul

Under the influence of British groups, a European sensibility had entered rock. Dylan and his contemporaries had developed their music in the heavily intellectual atmosphere of New York coffee houses. Folk-rock and Sixties R&B often consciously overshot their Southern

ancestry in laying claim to even deeper roots in European or African folk music. And, to top it all, rock had achieved a respectability and artistic credibility signalled by reviews in 'quality' newspapers, performances in opera houses and praise from 'radical chic' circles in America and Europe.

The raunchy, teen-obsessed, extrovert burst of energy that was Fifties rock'n'roll had given way to more politically aware and introspective meditations. The album market had grown considerably, and performers, critics and record executives alike talked of 'art rock', 'the poetry of rock' and 'rock as the cultural expression of a generation'. The South still pursued the old rock'n'roll formula that pitted restless energy against the thoughtfulness of so much of the music that emerged in the Sixties. Most spectacularly, it had the Muscle Shoals' studio in Florence, Alabama, and the Stax label in Memphis. These produced a variety of soul sounds featuring such artists as Percy Sledge, Joe Tex, Otis Redding and Booker T. and the MGs. (Later, TK Records of Hialeah, Florida, gave disco-funk a boost with records by Betty Wright, George McCrae and KC and the Sunshine Band.)

Most of the musicians working for these record companies were, in fact, white but, despite that, and despite the growing acceptance of country-rock, the South had, by the end of the Sixties, come to represent something totally alien to – and despised by – the mass of the rock audience. Kennedy had been killed there, as had Martin Luther King, and, in 1968, the man most reviled by the young of America was Texan president Lyndon B. Johnson.

Larry Hagman (above) starred as the unscrupulous J.R. Ewing in the popular TV series 'Dallas' – a dubious symbol of the new Southern prosperity. Creedence Clearwater Revival (below) were actually from San Francisco, but sought their inspiration in the swamplands.

The low point of the South's reputation was reached in 1969 with the film *Easy Rider*, which rode to worldwide success on its portrayal of what was effectively a state-of-war between hippie, acid-head rock-freaks and conservative, narrow-minded and vindictive Southerners. The film also demonstrated that, in their persistent 'searching for America', the rock-freaks were just as obsessed with tradition and the American identity as were their Southern redneck enemies.

Pseudo South

One of the goals in America's constant search for identity is the simplicity of an unbroken tradition. This quest is underlined in the names of the heroes in *Easy Rider* (Captain America and Billy the Kid), in the rediscovery of country music by the Byrds (under the guidance of Gram Parsons, born in Florida but brought up in Georgia and New Orleans) and in the pursuit of a mythic America swathed in the corn-gold glory of the time-honoured rural verities of independence, stoicism, good humour and fellowship.

Thus in the late Sixties, when America seemed to be moving towards hippiedom and art rock, it was perhaps inevitable that there should be a reverse movement – something concerned with traditional America, and, perhaps naturally, the South. But this was not the *real* South – it was the South of the *mind*, the South as seen from Berkeley. It was the *idea* of the South that gripped the imagination of those seeking refuge from a world grown over-complicated. Rockers seeking their 'roots' thus found them in a Memphis and New Orleans of their own invention.

After the Byrds, a San Francisco band called Creedence Clearwater Revival, with a succession of tight, three-minute singles with titles such as 'Proud Mary', 'Born On The Bayou', 'Bad Moon Rising' and 'Up Around The Bend', evoked images of river boats, Louisiana swamps and gambling men. Others took up the formula. Bob Dylan's backing group, the Band – with Levon Helm from Arkansas and the rest from Canada – played to the gallery with numbers like 'Cripple Creek', 'The Night They Drove Old Dixie Down', 'King Harvest' and 'Across The Great Divide'. Delaney Bramlett, a gospel-influenced guitarist from Mississippi, and Bonnie Lynn, who had recorded in Memphis, formed Delaney and Bonnie and Friends (among the friends were Eric Clapton, Dave Mason and George Harrison) to play what Delaney called 'a country sort of gospel'.

Session man Leon Russell (from Oklahoma) worked with them, as did Rita Coolidge and Joe Cocker – among others – in pursuit of a similar, but choral-inflected gospel sound. One of the biggest Russell-directed hits of the time was Joe Cocker's 'Delta Lady' (the delta being that of the Mississippi). Another session man, Joe South (from Atlanta) had a smash hit under his own name in 1969 with 'Games People Play' – a 'Southern hypocrisy' song in the same vein as Jeannie C. Riley's 'Harper Valley PTA' and Bobby Charles' later 'Small Town Talk'. Yet another session man, Mac Rebennack, emerged in 1968 as Dr John with a sound that cleverly combined the voodoo chants and R&B of his New Orleans hometown.

The Allman Brothers Band (above) were one of the pillars of the new Southern rock music, along with husband-and-wife duo Delaney and Bonnie Bramlett (left).

Then, of course, there were the Allman Brothers, born in Nashville, who moved to Los Angeles and then to Florida before settling in Macon, Georgia. They gave up psychedelia in the late Sixties, changing their name from Hourglass, to create the closest thing to an electrified country blues there has been in rock.

Rockin' the White House

The image that went along with it – somewhere between outlaws, farmers and patrician slave-owners – was perhaps the definitive statement of 'new' Southern values. Signing to Capricorn in Macon – a label owned by Phil Walden, the white manager of black artists including Clarence Carter and Percy Sledge – the Allmans became the hub of a small family of bands pursuing much the same sound and goal. Their identification with the New South was completed when it was revealed that Georgia state governor Jimmy Carter was a friend of Walden. Benefit concerts from Walden's stable of bands later boosted Carter's Presidential campaign.

By the mid Seventies, Southern rock had come into its own. Florida-based band Lynyrd Skynyrd answered Neil Young's *Easy Rider*-era attack on Southern values, 'Southern Man', with their 1975 hit 'Sweet Home Alabama'. A couple of years later, Jimmy Carter (then US president) invited the Atlanta Rhythm Section to play at the White House, and the South suddenly had a whole host of rock musicians to stand alongside Burt Reynolds, J. R. Ewing, Coca Cola and Silicon Valley as symbols of its curious victory over the North.   GARY HERMAN

LEON RUSSELL

From Asylum Choir to the Mad Dogs tour

THE IMPORTANCE OF the piano in rock was undeniably established by Fats Domino and Jerry Lee Lewis, but it is sometimes forgotten that Leon Russell was a vital catalyst in its rise to prominence. This neglect is probably due to Russell's withdrawn offstage personality. His deep, brooding intensity often scared those who didn't know him well, but it was the key to his musical genius. In 1971 Russell stated, revealingly, that he'd learned to play the piano by imagining himself 'lashed to a speedboat heading towards a rock'. One mistake and he would crash. This kind of fanaticism made him a technical master; it also made him, at times, difficult for others to understand.

Russell was born on 2 April 1941 in Lawton, Oklahoma, and emerged during the late Fifties playing white gospel piano and rock guitar. He was part of a small circle of musicians – David Gates, the late Carl Radle, Johnny (now J.J.) Cale – who developed their own kind of rockabilly on the Kansas/Oklahoma borders and went on to become internationally known musicians in other styles. Russell was a vital part of this local 'Tulsa Bop' and his expertise led to gigs with Ronnie Hawkins' band, the Hawks. He also played piano on David Gates' records for East-West, for the Strangers on KCM and on Jerry Adams' sides for the Oklahoma Wheel label.

His own recordings, made in 1959 under the name of Russell Bridges, showcased his frantic Jerry Lee Lewis piano style. 'Swanee River' and 'All Right', cut at Oklahoma's WKY radio station and leased to Chess, surfaced on various rockabilly compilations in the Seventies. During the early Sixties Russell played briefly in Jerry Lee Lewis' road band. By 1962, he had moved to Los Angeles where he obtained work as a full-time session pianist. He played on Walter Brennan's Top Five hit, 'Old Rivers', and on numerous sessions for Phil Spector (the Crystals, Ronettes, Righteous Brothers) as well as Herb Alpert and Terry Melcher (who fixed sessions with the Byrds). Russell went completely commercial in 1965 to work on most of the biggest hits produced by Gary Lewis and the Playboys. This move did little for his professional reputation as a performer, but it must have increased his studio experience as a record producer as well as boosting his bank balance.

In 1966, Gary Lewis was drafted and sent to Vietnam. A year later, producer Snuff Garrett recommended Russell to write and produce for Harpers Bizarre. Their first album was a tremendous success, and 'Feelin' Groovy', which Russell had arranged, hit the top of the US charts in just a few months.

'Misty' mistake

With the money made from Gary Lewis and the Harpers, Russell produced his own first record – an uptempo, C&W version of Errol Garner's 'Misty' – in 1965. The style was at odds with the material, and the combination didn't work. The disc was issued as a single and reappeared later on the first *A&M Bootleg Album.* The failure of 'Misty' was a setback for Russell, both financially and in terms of his career. But his prospects began to improve when he teamed up with a husband-and-wife duo whose musical ideals coincided with his own. This was Delaney and Bonnie Bramlett – a unique combination of his laid-back country-soul style and her full-blooded white blues.

Their first album together was *Accept No Substitute* (1969). Delaney and Russell arranged the entire album, and the latter's piano is heard prominently. This album records Russell's first meeting with the members of the group that was later to become Mad Dogs and Englishmen. It also marked Russell's first public appearance with his lover, Rita Coolidge. What she meant to him in terms of moral and artistic support cannot be over-estimated. She was with him at the peak of his career; she inspired him to some of his finest achievements; and when she left him in 1972 his music lost much of its frenetic energy.

Touring with the Bramletts gave Russell the opportunity to work on one of his greatest sessions. While in California, he met Marc Benno, an accomplished folk-rock performer. Benno was fired by Russell's neurotic energy; they worked together at the Skyhill Studios in Hollywood in the spring of 1968 and emerged with about an hour's worth of tape, which was edited down to 25 minutes and issued on the Smash label later that year as the *Asylum Choir* album.

This short album contains some of the most creative gospel-rock ever issued. From the very first track, 'Welcome To Hollywood', the listener is knocked out by the frantic energy of Russell's piano and vocals and the power of his guitar work. Benno is featured on guitar, bass and

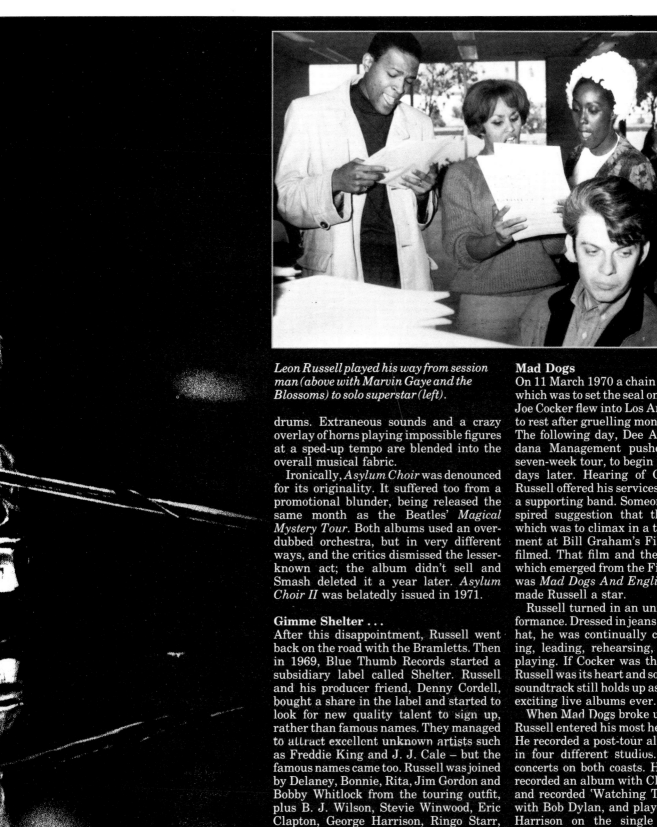

Leon Russell played his way from session man (above with Marvin Gaye and the Blossoms) to solo superstar (left).

drums. Extraneous sounds and a crazy overlay of horns playing impossible figures at a sped-up tempo are blended into the overall musical fabric.

Ironically, *Asylum Choir* was denounced for its originality. It suffered too from a promotional blunder, being released the same month as the Beatles' *Magical Mystery Tour*. Both albums used an over-dubbed orchestra, but in very different ways, and the critics dismissed the lesser-known act; the album didn't sell and Smash deleted it a year later. *Asylum Choir II* was belatedly issued in 1971.

Gimme Shelter . . .

After this disappointment, Russell went back on the road with the Bramletts. Then in 1969, Blue Thumb Records started a subsidiary label called Shelter. Russell and his producer friend, Denny Cordell, bought a share in the label and started to look for new quality talent to sign up, rather than famous names. They managed to attract excellent unknown artists such as Freddie King and J. J. Cale – but the famous names came too. Russell was joined by Delaney, Bonnie, Rita, Jim Gordon and Bobby Whitlock from the touring outfit, plus B. J. Wilson, Stevie Winwood, Eric Clapton, George Harrison, Ringo Starr, Klaus Voorman, Charlie Watts, Bill Wyman, Joe Cocker and Chris Stainton for the recording of his first solo album. It was the first time most of them had worked with Russell in the studio, but they were inspired by his dedication and the talent flashed like lightning.

Russell wrote all but one of the songs, including 'Delta Lady', written about Coolidge, and 'A Song For You'; both became rock classics. Cordell quickly arranged a tour to plug *Leon Russell*, and it was acclaimed by the critics.

Mad Dogs

On 11 March 1970 a chain of events began which was to set the seal on Russell's fame. Joe Cocker flew into Los Angeles planning to rest after gruelling months on the road. The following day, Dee Anthony of Bandana Management pushed him into a seven-week tour, to begin in Detroit eight days later. Hearing of Cocker's plight, Russell offered his services in rounding up a supporting band. Someone made the inspired suggestion that the entire tour, which was to climax in a two-day engagement at Bill Graham's Fillmore East, be filmed. That film and the two-record set which emerged from the Fillmore concerts was *Mad Dogs And Englishmen* – and it made Russell a star.

Russell turned in an unforgettable performance. Dressed in jeans, T-shirt and top hat, he was continually coaching, cheering, leading, rehearsing, arranging and playing. If Cocker was the group's head, Russell was its heart and soul. The original soundtrack still holds up as one of the most exciting live albums ever.

When Mad Dogs broke up in May 1970, Russell entered his most hectic 18 months. He recorded a post-tour album on Shelter in four different studios. He performed concerts on both coasts. He co-wrote and recorded an album with Clapton, co-wrote and recorded 'Watching The River Flow' with Bob Dylan, and played with George Harrison on the single 'Bangla-Desh', which he also produced. On 12 August 1971 he was one of the stars in a mammoth concert at New York's Madison Square Garden as a benefit for Bangladesh. At the top of his form, Russell gave stunning performances of 'Jumpin' Jack Flash' and 'Young Blood'. The concert was recorded and filmed.

Russell was a performer in demand, and the future looked promising. But then legal troubles beset Shelter Records when National Comics sued them for copying their trademark, an inverted Superman 'S' on an eggshell. Russell and Cordell fought a bitter battle, and eventually lost.

Further trouble was in store for Russell. In early 1972 on a visit to Britain to play with Stainton and Clapton, it was reported that he had suffered a nervous breakdown. The 18 months of work and stress had taken their toll even on this most energetic of performers. Many feared he'd never perform again; or, if he did, that it wouldn't be the same.

His first album after recovery, *Carney*, would have been considered a fine achievement coming from any other artist; indeed, it reached Number 2 in the US album charts in 1972. But to some of his followers, Russell's new mellowness betrayed a weakness of spirit, an admission of defeat from a man who was sick of the financial and political side of the music business. As

he sang in the hit single from the album, 'Tight Rope': 'I'm on a high wire/One side's life, and one is fire/But the top hat on my head is all you see.'

Country and jazz

After 1972 Russell's music reflected the steady and calming influence of Mary McCreery, who became his wife, though he still continued to explore alternative

Although Leon Russell will be remembered for the ferocious, driving energy of his piano playing (inset below right), he was also an able and effective guitarist (right). His guitar-playing was amply demonstrated when he appeared at London's Rainbow Theatre in 1972 (inset below left), sharing the stage with Eric Clapton once again two years after the Mad Dogs tour.

musical styles. The albums of this period include *Leon Live* (1973), his second Top Ten album, the country LP *Hank Wilson Is Back* (also 1973), *Stop All That Jazz* (1974) and his venture into soul with Mary, *Make Love To The Music* (1977). He has subsequently performed on television with her and an old friend, country-and-western star Willie Nelson.

Russell's career falls into two distinct phases – before and after his breakdown, the first phase being more spontaneous and creative, and the second lacking in the drive and lustre that used to be his trademark. The energy of Russell's music during the earlier period had the explosive impact of a train hurtling out of a tunnel. And that's something which, on record at least, the listener can treasure forever.

STEPHEN M STROFF

Leon Russell
Recommended Listening

Leon Russell (A&M AMLS 982) (Includes: A Song For You, I Put A Spell On You, Hummingbird, Roll Away The Stone, Delta Lady, Dixie Lullaby); *Leon Russell And The Shelter People* (A&M AMLS 65003) (Includes: Stranger In A Strange Land, Home Sweet Oklahoma, It Takes A Lot To Laugh It Takes A Train To Cry, A Hard Rain's A-Gonna Fall, Of Thee I Sing, Sweet Emily).

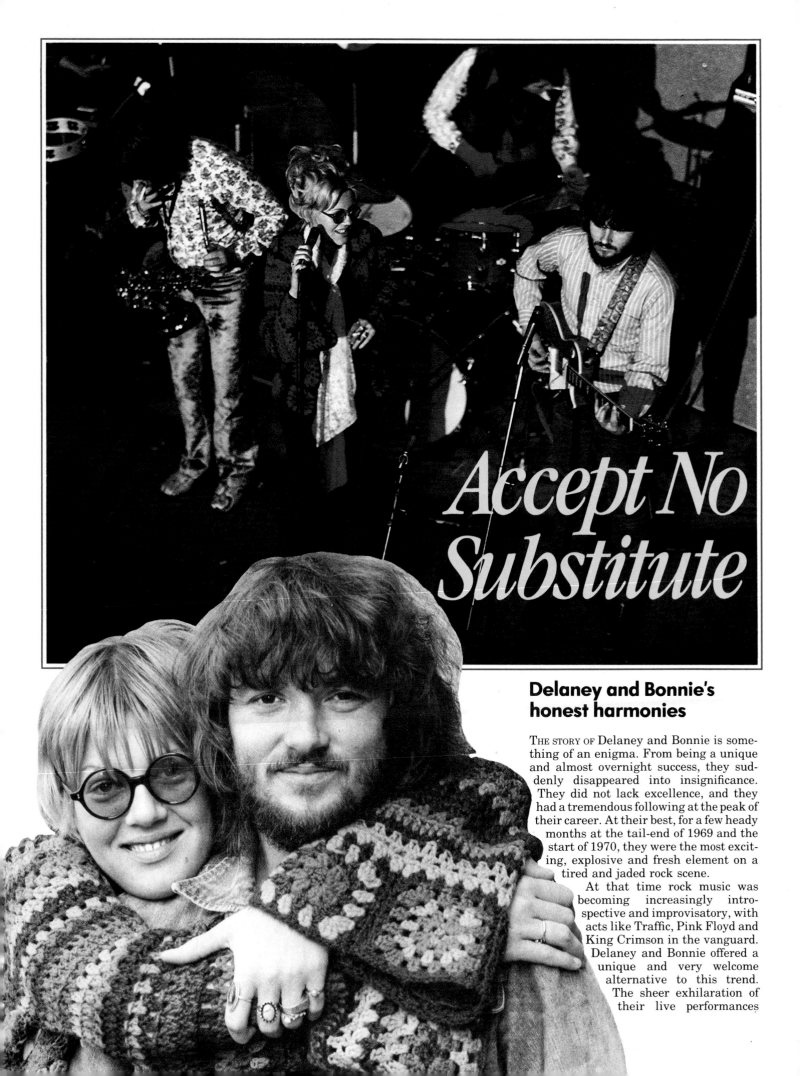

Accept No Substitute

Delaney and Bonnie's honest harmonies

THE STORY OF Delaney and Bonnie is something of an enigma. From being a unique and almost overnight success, they suddenly disappeared into insignificance. They did not lack excellence, and they had a tremendous following at the peak of their career. At their best, for a few heady months at the tail-end of 1969 and the start of 1970, they were the most exciting, explosive and fresh element on a tired and jaded rock scene.

At that time rock music was becoming increasingly introspective and improvisatory, with acts like Traffic, Pink Floyd and King Crimson in the vanguard. Delaney and Bonnie offered a unique and very welcome alternative to this trend. The sheer exhilaration of their live performances set them apart from their self-absorbed peers. From the Beatles downwards, the rock business was momentarily captivated by them. Here, it was felt, was the act that could really put contemporary music back on the rock'n'roll rails.

The only group that had a comparable influence was Creedence Clearwater Revival – but, as their name implied, they were really revivalists, whereas Delaney and Bonnie, with an act that was a potent blend of soul, gospel and rock, seemed to be forging a new path. Indeed, they were inheritors of a blue-eyed soul tradition that began with the Righteous Brothers in 1964. It was hardly their fault that, as the Seventies progressed, the term acquired increasingly pejorative connotations.

Bowled over

Delaney Bramlett was born in Randolph, Mississippi, on 1 July 1939, and spent three years in the US Navy before leaving to try his luck in the rock business. He was particularly impressed by Jack Good's US television show, 'Shindig', and teamed with Joey Cooper formed the Shindogs, who became residents on the programme. They left the show in 1967, and in the same year Delaney met Bonnie Lynn while playing the Carolina Lanes Bowling Alley in Los Angeles. Five days later, they were married. Bonnie (born 8 November 1944) had grown up in Granite City, Illinois, and at the age of 15 she was singing in jazz clubs in St Louis. By the time she met Delaney, she had served a valuable apprenticeship as a backing vocalist for Fontella Bass and Albert King, and had also become the first white member of Ike and Tina Turner's Ikettes.

Delaney and Bonnie put together a quite remarkable backing group which, for want of a better name, they referred to simply as the Friends. One of the first people with whom Delaney had become acquainted in Los Angeles was Leon Russell; he readily joined the band and helped to give it a strong Oklahoma flavour by bringing in bassist Carl Radle and the then-unknown J. J. Cale on guitar.

Over the course of the next two years other recruits were added – Jim Keltner, Bobby Whitlock, Jim Price, Bobby Keys and Rita Coolidge. Delaney and Bonnie had made their initial recording efforts without the powerful support of the Friends, however, and in both cases the tapes were shelved until after the duo's precipitate rise to fame.

The reputation of the Friends remained confined for some time to Los Angeles, where they were giving increasingly mature and exuberant performances. Although they came to the attention of celebrities such as George Harrison, the troupe were barely making ends meet because there were so many of them.

Things began to change in 1969 when, in the summer, they were signed to Elektra Records and, in September, joined the Blind Faith US tour. By that time, they had recorded *Accept No Substitute*, the title of which was a fair reflection of the charisma already surrounding the band. Produced by David Anderle, the album successfully captured the fire and fervour of their music. It was to prove the best Delaney and Bonnie album.

Influential friends

By the time the Blind Faith tour started, J. J. Cale had quit, but the Friends, though third on the bill, proved a great attraction – so much so that Eric Clapton was caught up in the excitement. He had already left Cream to change musical direction and now he left Blind Faith to change direction again. His contribution proved invaluable – not only did he volunteer his services as a Friend, he also arranged to co-promote a UK and European tour for the group in conjunction with his manager, Robert Stigwood.

Opposite: Delaney and Bonnie on stage (top) and in marital bliss (below). Above: George Harrison (top left) and Eric Clapton (centre) were among the Bramletts' backing musicians in 1969.

Despite the support of such a prominent personality as Clapton, Elektra expected so little from these dates that they didn't release *Accept No Substitute* in Britain. George Harrison quickly snapped up the UK rights for the Beatles' Apple label, and even arranged to appear with the Friends on several dates. But though Clapton's presence was well advertised, Harrison's was strictly unannounced due to his personal reticence: he played rhythm guitar in the background. Because of the lack of publicity, some concert halls were only half-full for the early dates, but after a fortnight audience reaction was so positive that the show built up its own momentum, and Delaney and Bonnie were drawing capacity crowds.

A single, 'Comin' Home', made the UK Top Twenty, and tapes of another date at Croydon were released as a live album, *On Tour*. This was their most successful album, reaching Number 29 in the US album chart in 1970.

At this stage, it would have been easy to predict that Delaney and Bonnie's tremendous following would assure them superstardom for years to come. But what happened was that virtually everybody connected with the show achieved considerable fame during the following year – with the ironic exception of Delaney and Bonnie.

After playing some promising US dates, the Bramletts lost almost their entire band to Leon Russell, who was putting together a group to help out Joe Cocker on what became the Mad Dogs and Englishmen extravaganza. That tour became one of the most famous of all time, and received precisely the kind of acclaim that Delaney and Bonnie should have generated for their own concerts.

Parting shot

Bonnie was particularly bitter about the events of 1970, but she and Delaney were not immediately becalmed. The duo released *To Bonnie From Delaney*, which had moments of great inspiration, including a blistering version of 'Miss Ann', which featured a characteristically frenetic performance from Little Richard. After that came *Motel Shot*, which was somewhat disappointing, though *Together* recouped most of the duo's strengths.

In the end, marital disharmony destroyed any lingering hopes of a real commercial breakthrough, despite the occasional hit single; 'Never Ending Song Of Love' made the US Number 13 position in 1971. By the time they moved to CBS in the following year, one of the most promising double acts of 1969 had become two unexceptional solo performers.

So what went wrong? Apart from the disastrous loss of their band, two other difficulties are apparent. The first is that their style remained static and that there was no musical progression. Secondly there was the fact that their first four albums all appeared on different labels, so that Elektra had little incentive to promote *Accept No Substitute*, which was their best release.

After their breakup, neither Delaney nor Bonnie achieved much as a solo performer. Delaney was contracted to Tamla Motown's Prodigal label in 1977, and recorded *Class Reunion* with several old Friends, including Clapton and Harrison, but the album sank without trace. Bonnie had a slice of ill-luck when she signed to Capricorn shortly before the company collapsed. Later, she attracted some publicity through a liaison with Stephen Stills. After becoming a born-again Christian in 1980, she released a powerful gospel album, but it was much underrated.

BOB WOFFINDEN

Delaney And Bonnie
Recommended Listening

Accept No Substitute (Elektra EKS 74039)
(Includes: Get Ourselves Together, The Ghetto, Love Me A Little Bit Longer, I Can't Take It Much Longer, Soldiers Of The Cross, Gift Of Love).

NIGHT TRIPPER

Dr John: medicine man or high priest of voodoo?

MALCOLM JOHN MICHAEL Creaux Rebennack, better known as Dr John, is an integral part of the unsurpassable New Orleans tradition of high-class funk. He is one of the Crescent City's great stylists, and his keyboard playing embodies the vital sound of an area that has yielded such unimpeachable musicians as Fats Domino, Professor Longhair, James Booker and Allen Toussaint. Dr John's story touches on so many parts of the local sound that his career virtually reads like a one-man almanac of the richest American musical tradition of all.

Session student
Born in New Orleans on 21 November 1940, he started listening to hillbilly music in his father's Garden District record store before graduating to the role of guitarist on countless sessions in the late Fifties and early Sixties. After learning his technique from Fats Domino's guitarist Walter Nelson, the teenage Rebennack sat in on sessions with saxophonist Lee Allen and contributed often uncredited parts for

Above: A late Fifties Mac Rebennack twangs his Telecaster. Opposite: A decade later, bizarre headwear and make-up have transformed him into Dr John Creaux the Night Tripper.

records on the Ace, Rex and Ebb labels. Mac played guitar on records by Professor Longhair, Huey Smith, Jimmy Clanton, Joe Tex, Frankie Ford and Charles Brown. He wrote 'Lights Out' for Jerry Byrne, 'What's Going On' for Art Neville, 'Losing Battle' for Johnny Adams and 'Lady Luck', which, pirated by Lloyd Price, reached the US Top Twenty in 1960.

Mac Rebennack cut his own debut disc, a Bo Diddley-styled guitar instrumental called 'Storm Warning', in 1959 and he subsequently recorded as Morgus and the Three Ghouls for the Vin label, under his own name for Ace and with Ronnie Barron as Drits and Dravy. By the early Sixties, he had become part of a pool of players (which included Booker and Toussaint) that the noted arranger Harold Battiste would call on to play on his All For One, a co-operative label that encouraged the cream of the area to back singers like Barbara George and Prince La La. Mac continued to work both as A&R man and journeyman writer, but the sheer abundance of talent in New Orleans at the time, not to mention the very nature of the star system then, made it hard for a musician to gain individual recognition.

More sinister was the racism endemic in the Southern music scene, where it was still considered unacceptable for black and white musicians to play together. Backing various singers, Rebennack would often be the only white man in the group. In doing this, he was skating thin ice with the players, all of whom needed to toe their union line to stay in business. The rigid rule of the unions and the thriving trade in bootleg recordings was accompanied by some highly unscrupulous dealings that affected Rebennack directly when he was shot through the hand in a bar-room brawl. He promptly moved out of town on the advice of some gangsters who probably didn't have his best interests at heart.

A step in the dark

Settling in Los Angeles, Mac rejoined Battiste to play on Sonny and Cher sessions. He also produced Jesse Hill and Shirley Goodman, and recorded for A&M under the name of the Zu Zu Blues Band. After being, on his own admission, 'severely strung out' for several years, Rebennack secured a deal with Atlantic, for whom he signed under the name Dr John Creaux the Night Tripper. The title of 'Dr' was inspired by Professor Longhair, while 'the Night Tripper' was an answer to the Beatles' 'Day Tripper'.

His career thereafter falls into distinct phases. The LPs *Gris Gris* (1968), *Babylon* (1969), *Remedies* (1970) and *Sun, Moon And Herbs* (1971) are notable for his mumbled incantations against hypnotic voodoo-inspired settings. 'Walk On Gilded Splinters' from *Gris Gris* was covered by Humble Pie, Johnny Jenkins and Marsha Hunt. Dr John became a fashionable figure, patronised by the likes of Mick Jagger and Eric Clapton, both of whom appeared on *Sun, Moon And Herbs*.

Dr John's next LP saw a drastic change of direction. *Gumbo* (1972), a tribute to the musicians of New Orleans, played down the 'voodoo' mannerisms – which were probably an artful contrivance intended to hoodwink gullible hippies and music journalists – in favour of an honest, rootsy R&B approach. One track off the album, 'Iko Iko', also gave Mac Rebennack his first hit single, reaching Number 71 in the US charts in April 1972. He toured Europe twice in the early Seventies, latterly with Allen Toussaint and the Meters. This revelatory musical experience probably brought the sound of Louisiana to a wider audience than any tour apart from those by Fats Domino.

Last tango in Hollywood

The third phase of the Dr John story found him working in harmony with Toussaint on *In The Right Place* (1973) and *Destively Bonaroo* (1974). As on *Gumbo*, Mac now displayed confidence to vocalise a lyric rather than use his throat as a spell-casting instrument. He was also concentrating on his highly economical yet soulful keyboard technique, fleshing out the sound with two intriguing instruments called the zigola and the muted fingernettes.

Despite the popularity of these albums (the first of which spawned two successful singles in 'Right Place, Wrong Time' and 'Such A Night'), Mac Rebennack parted company with Atlantic soon after and entered the fourth phase of his career, since when he has recorded infrequently, although *Hollywood Be Thy Name* (1975), *Tango Palace* (1979) and *Plays Mac Rebennack* (1982) are proof that there has been no dilution of his extraordinary talent.

Although Mac performed rarely in the early Eighties, he could still be seen at the New Orleans annual Jazz Heritage Festival, beguiling the faithful with his hallucinatory music, spells, incense and his bizarre costume of beads, head-dress and flowing astronomer's robes. He was, as always, a strangely compelling figure, playing to the hilt the part of Dr John . . . the Night Tripper. MAX BELL

Above: Dr John tickles the ivories in the late Seventies. Below: On stage, Rebennack beguiles the faithful.

**Dr John
Recommended Listening**

Gris Gris (Atlantic 588147) (Includes: Gris-Gris
Gumbo Ya Ya, Mama Roux, Jump Sturdy, Danse
Fambeaux, Croker Courtbullion); *Sun, Moon And
Herbs* (Atlantic 2400 161) (Black John The
Conqueror, Where Ya At Mule, Craney Crow,
Familiar Reality).

SOUNDS *of the* SWAMP

Local heroes who rocked the everglades

FOUR HUNDRED MILES of US highway run between Port Arthur, Texas in the West and New Orleans, Louisiana in the East. On either side of it are found the townships of South Louisiana and all the smaller settlements that spring to life in the songs and stories of cajun or swamp-pop. There are Lake Charles and Ville Platte, the home of

Floyd Soileau's Jin and Swallow labels; Abbeville, where Bobby Charles lives in hermit-like seclusion; Crowley, where Jay Miller recorded the finest Excello blues, and such outposts of swampland as the aptly-named Cut Off, Joe Barry's home.

Between 1958 and 1962, the US charts were alive with the sound of white singers and musicians from all these places. Five of the most influential were Joe Barry, Jivin' Gene, T. K. Hulin, Warren Storm and Rod Bernard, and for a brief period they captivated American record-buyers with a strange, eerie sound that was indigenous to south Louisiana, but alien to the general mainstream of popular music. The critics have called it swamp-pop, cajun-rock or bayou-beat, but to the locals it is simply south Louisiana music. Johnnie Allan, a singer whose local popularity has endured for 25 years, says: 'I guess the only way to describe it is to say that it's the musicians who make the sound different. Those guys, Jivin' Gene, T. K. Hulin – virtually all of them speak French. Their family names are French and some of them played in French accordion bands just like I did. Consequently, I think we all kept part of this French-cajun music ingrained in us; you can detect it, something of a cajun flavour in the song.'

Local colour

The cajuns of south-west Louisiana are unique. Banished from Nova Scotia, the French settlers arrived in Louisiana in the 1760s and developed a distinctive and colourful music in virtual isolation. Cajun followers differentiate between traditional music – played on accordion, fiddle, rhythm guitar and triangle, with vocals in a French patois – and a more progressive but still authentic strain with a marked hillbilly influence, which can have the fiddle leading instead of the accordion.

The name of Joe Falcon, who made the first cajun records during the late Twenties, is synonymous with traditional cajun, while in the Eighties most South Louisiana groups play in the modern authentic style. A third category, pop- or

Far left: Southern swampland – Atchafalaya basin, Louisiana. The sound of swamp-pop and bayou-beat is typified by the work of singers Warren Storm (opposite), Johnnie Allan (above) and cajun producer Floyd Soileau (top).

Nashville-cajun, embraces Jimmy Newman and the Kershaw Brothers, musicians who strive for national recognition without losing their local identity. The best-known song from this third group is Rusty and Doug Kershaw's 'Louisiana Man', which boasts over 400 recordings. It evokes images of local life, describing muskrat skins drying in the sun and web-footed children named Ned or Mack who fish from a canoe called a pirogue and accompany Papa Jack on his trips to town.

Swamp-pop was born of many things. The first variation of it to reach the Hot Hundred was influenced as much by the intensity of early Elvis and the music of Fats Domino as the original French cajun style of Joseph Falcon. This batch of music was typified by Warren Storm's 'Prisoner's Song', which became a best seller in 1958, and Rod Bernard's 'This Should Go On Forever', which reached the US Top Twenty the following year. Although Fats Domino's infectious piano triplets and

clipped vocals were particularly pervasive, meandering songs of other black New Orleans artists, Guitar Slim ('The Things I Used To Do') and Earl King ('Those Lonely Lonely Nights'), contributed much to the structure of swamp-pop. '"Those Lonely Lonely Nights",' explained Dr John, 'is a classic South Louisiana two-chord – E flat, B flat – slow ballad.'

The same simple chord progressions characterised most swamp-pop and, although whites enjoyed a greater success with this musical hybrid, black artists like Phil Phillips, whose 'Sea Of Love' reached Number Two in 1959, Elton Anderson and Cookie and the Cupcakes were prime exponents of the style. Cookie, otherwise Huey Thierry from Jennings, Louisiana, had got together a collection of local musicians including Shelton Dunaway, a vibrant singer whose voice was characteristic of the genre.

The 'Crazy Cajun'

Tiny, one-man record labels have always existed in south Louisiana towns, but aspiring swamp-rockers generally signed with Mercury, a label that had nationwide distribution. Mercury proved it could have, hits with Southern music, and local producers Huey Meaux, George Khoury and Floyd Soileau developed strong ties with this major company. Meaux worked mostly in Texas and Mississippi although he was born in Kaplan, Louisiana and is widely known as the 'Crazy Cajun'. He first recorded Jivin' Gene in Port Arthur in 1959 and East Texas/South Louisiana sounds have characterised much of what he produced thereafter, including Freddy Fender's major hits of the mid Seventies, 'Before The Next Teardrop Falls' and 'Wasted Days And Wasted Nights'.

Floyd Soileau, who distributes almost every cajun label and produces a high percentage of cajun records on his own, is no less dedicated to what he calls 'south Louisiana rock'n'roll'. Like most Southern record producers, he had no wish to expand to compete with the nationals, and when a disc of his began to attract sales outside Louisiana, he automatically placed the master with a major label: Johnnie Allan's 'Lonely Days And Lonely Nights' (MGM), Joe Barry's 'I'm A Fool To Care' (Smash) and Rod Bernard's 'This Should Go On Forever' (Argo) were all Soileau's records, as was Tommy McLain's 1966 million-seller 'Sweet Dreams' (MSL).

These unexpected, even accidental breakthroughs into the pop field have since become few and far between but, while authentic swamp-pop has been relegated to the backwaters of pop appreciation, its echoes linger on in the laments of Dr John, Chas and Dave ('Ain't No Pleasing You') and Doug Sahm. Locally, there's an insatiable demand for new versions of swamp-pop favourites. Unaffected by the often bizarre musical fashions of the day, swamp-pop remains a living tradition from which young and old continue to draw strength and inspiration.   BILL MILLAR

TRAVELIN' BAND

'SAN FRANCISCO ROCK GROUPS are now the dominant force in a popular music which is the most universal expression of attitudes and ideas we've ever seen,' wrote Ralph J. Gleason in the sleeve notes of Creedence Clearwater Revival's first album. 'Creedence Clearwater Revival is an excellent example of the Third Generation of San Francisco bands which gives every indication of keeping the strength of the San Francisco sound undiminished.'

Yet Creedence was very much more than just another San Francisco band – in fact the only thing they had in common with their contemporaries was geography. For whereas the prevailing trend in late-Sixties West Coast rock was toward psychedelic exploration, radical hippie sloganeering and complex 'progressive' fare, Creedence drew their inspiration from Fifties rock'n'roll, country and R&B, and their leader, John Fogerty, would later be recognised as a consummate stylist and all-round exponent of rock'n'roll's most enduring strongpoints. The group's great achievement was in appealing to pop and rock fans alike – their success in both the singles and albums market was phenomenal – and in this they were unique.

Were Creedence the Hot Hundred's fastest movers?

Creedence Clearwater Revival were two guitar-playing brothers, John Fogerty (born Berkeley, 28 May 1945) and Tom Fogerty (born 9 November 1941), bassist Stu Cook (born Oakland, 25 April 1945) and drummer Doug Clifford (born Palo Alto, 24 April 1945). They started playing rock'n'roll together during the late Fifties while attending high school in El Cerrito, a suburb of San Francisco's East Bay area.

By the time of the British beat invasion, the group were called the Blue Velvets, playing a mixture of current hit material and cutting their teeth on various Fifties rock'n'roll standards. As such they may well have remained in obscurity on the wrong side of the Bay had not record com-

Below, from left: Tom Fogerty, John Fogerty, Doug 'Cosmo' Clifford and Stu Cook. Despite their indefinable image, Creedence Clearwater Revival were to prove equally successful with the divided camps of singles buyers and progressive rock album fans.

panies, fired by the success of the Beatles, been on the lookout for guitar groups of their own. As it was, in 1964 the Blue Velvets, who had released one flop single on the Orchestra label, auditioned for the local Fantasy label and were signed on condition they change their name to something more in keeping with the current beat trend.

As the Golliwogs, a name chosen by Fantasy, much to the group's embarrassment, they were to release seven singles on Fantasy and its affiliated Scorpio label. And while none of the records were hits, it's possible to trace the developing expertise and style of the band from the straight Beatles imitation, 'Don't Tell Me No Lies', through the rough-edged garage punk of 'Brown Eyed Girl' to the more refined and original 'Fight Fire' and 'Walking On The Water'.

Initially, Tom Fogerty had been responsible for most of the group's vocals and lead guitar work, but by the time of 'Brown Eyed Girl' younger brother John had taken charge of both departments, relegating Tom to rhythm. And in addition, John Fogerty would soon be writing most of the band's material.

On Christmas Eve 1967 the Golliwogs put paid to their tenuous and by now long outdated links with British beat and rechristened themselves Creedence Clearwater Revival, a name that evoked the southern swamplands of the bayou and the everglades. Their roots, or at least their hearts, lay in the raw blues-tinged sounds of the older musical capitals – Memphis, New Orleans, even Nashville. Creedence were an American band throughout but one that avoided the occasionally cloying self-consciousness of California brand leaders like the Beach Boys. Nor did they make a habit of paying lip-service to revolutionary cant.

With great encouragement from Saul Zaentz, who had bought Fantasy early in 1968 and who was a great believer in John Fogerty's talents, the group recorded their first album, *Creedence Clearwater Revival*, which was released in the early summer of 1968. The LP mixed standards, such as Screamin' Jay Hawkins' 'I Put A Spell On You' and Dale Hawkins' 'Suzie Q', with originals and, although John Fogerty's compositions lacked the maturity and confidence of his future offerings, the group's sound and performance were strong, fresh and original. The LP was greeted with much critical approval and sold surprisingly well for an unknown act, reaching Number 52 in the album charts. Later,

Above: On stage in Paris, 1970. Inset top: a poster for London concerts the same year. Inset above: 'Proud Mary keeps on rollin'' – and announces a new single release.

'Suzie Q' was released as a single and, in October, reached Number 11 in the singles charts.

Born on the Bayou
'Suzie Q' summed up Creedence's sound and musical formula perfectly; it was direct and instantly accessible, the churning, relentless rhythms of Cook, Clifford and Tom Fogerty providing an ideally simple backdrop for John's gravelly vocals and unmannered, vibrant guitar solos.

Apart from a version of 'Good Golly Miss Molly', all the songs on the group's next LP, *Bayou Country*, were written by John Fogerty, and they revealed, for the first time, his immense abilities. Released in January 1969, the album quickly reached Number 8 in the US LP charts while 'Proud Mary', a single drawn from the album, made it to Number 2. 'Proud Mary' rapidly established itself as a contemporary pop classic and was covered by Ike and Tina Turner, Solomon Burke and Elvis Presley among others.

With *Bayou Country*, it had become apparent that no other writer of the era could match Fogerty's mastery of rock,

soul and R&B. More important, his interpretative skills were allied to a unique vision that transformed the previously forgotten image of the 'devil's music' into something new and potent. Like Presley and Chuck Berry before him, Fogerty possessed both the imagination and the flair to generate recorded excitement and fuel a level of live energy that was missing in the more drawn out, narcotic excursions of the West Coast's other major outfits. Juke-boxes, radios and parties bore testimony to the Creedence appeal and Fogerty's seemingly inexhaustible supply of songs from the heartland, songs about trains, travelling, the promise of America and the failure.

Green River, released in August 1969, continued to increase Creedence Clearwater Revival's mass popularity, affording two massive hit singles in 'Bad Moon Rising' and the album's title track. Fogerty showed that he was not only a highly gifted writer but a prolific one, too, when in December Creedence released their third album of the year.

On *Willy And The Poor Boys*, John's romantic streak was balanced by a strong streak of reality, the LP benefiting from a core of social comment that was far more intelligent and tolerant than any futile call to arms. In particular, the song 'Fortunate Son' was an acutely powerful

rebuttal of privilege and authority, a song written in the voice and language of a working-class man with dignity and morals. Fogerty spoke out for the commoner, black or white, and his fight for welfare, a fair deal, a chance to escape the burden of grinding poverty and death-dealing patriotism.

'Fortunate Son' was the B-side of 'Down On The Corner', a jaunty, gospel-inflected number with an infectious backbeat, which reached Number 3 in the US charts in December 1969 and eventually sold more than a million copies. Singles success continued throughout 1970 – 'Travelin' Band' and 'Lookin' Out My Back Door' both reached Number 2, while 'Up Around The Bend' made it to Number 4.

The pendulum swings

These three singles were included on *Cosmo's Factory*, released in July, which remains possibly Creedence's finest album. It is the one that best indicates (particularly on the 11-minute version of 'I Heard It Through The Grapevine', which blended commercial directness with improvisation to perfect effect) the group's appeal to two distinct audiences – few, if any, other artists of the era were both teen-mag pin-ups and *Rolling Stone* interviewees.

After *Cosmo's Factory*, however, the rot began to set in. Somewhat inevitably for such a hugely commercial and successful band, rock critics began to turn against Creedence, suggesting they had nothing to offer but 'good-time' music. And, rather than ignoring the criticism, John Fogerty and group responded with *Pendulum*, an album on which they attempted to extend their basic formula to encompass more experimental arrangements and instrumentation. The chugging rhythm and biting lead guitar set-up which had, along with John Fogerty's grating voice, become trademarks of the Creedence sound, were now swamped by heavy-handed organ, saxes and vibes.

'*Cosmo's Factory* is what I consider to be the culmination of the whole thing,' John

Above: Doug Clifford sweats it out behind the kit. Inset above right: Stu Cook – in search of the lost chord? Inset far right: Tom Fogerty and white Guild guitar. Feeling overshadowed by his younger brother, Tom quit the group in 1971. Thereafter, Creedence continued to record and perform as a three-piece (right).

Fogerty told *Melody Maker* in 1974. 'My control of the band stopped somewhere in the middle of *Pendulum – Mardi Gras* was just out of the question.'

Released in April 1972, *Mardi Gras* proved to be Creedence Clearwater Revival's final album. Tom Fogerty had quit the band after *Pendulum* in February 1971 to pursue a solo career and John now gave in to the demands of the other band members for more artistic freedom. As a result, only three of the LP's 10 tracks were John Fogerty compositions, the remainder being written and sung by Clifford or Cook. Unfortunately, the composing abilities of the bassist and drummer were limited and paled into insignificance alongside those of Fogerty; although another million-seller, *Mardi Gras* was an artistic disaster.

Creedence Clearwater Revival now split up with good grace, having amassed seven gold albums and a fistful of hit singles in just four years. Individually, all erstwhile members continued to record. Clifford came up with a solo album, *Doug 'Cosmo' Clifford*, before teaming up once more with Stu Cook in the Don Harrison Band in 1976. Cook also moved into production, working with the bizarre figure of ex-Thirteenth Floor Elevators singer Roky Erickson. Tom Fogerty, meanwhile, showed a surprising taste and variety both on his own solo albums and with the band Ruby in the late Seventies.

Naturally enough, though, it is John Fogerty's solo excursions that repay the closest investigation. His first move, once free of Creedence, was to assemble a collection of his favourite country songs, acknowledging another influence that was always a part of his songwriting. The resulting collection was released in 1973

under the title of *The Blue Ridge Rangers*. The Rangers were a group with a difference, for Fogerty played, arranged, sang and produced every last note – yet there was none of the grating excess and lack of discernment that mars most other similar ventures. Instead Fogerty displayed his usual good judgement, mixing gospel with country laments, blues with ballads, rags with rich uptempo love songs (one element of popular songwriting he rarely attempted himself). Where a new instrument like keyboards, violin, banjo or steel guitar was called for, Fogerty simply learned it – yet his dedication was never academic; his interpretation was always honest and fresh.

On a second solo album, *John Fogerty* (1975), he returned to rock'n'roll, combining numbers like 'Sea Cruise' and 'Lonely

After the Creedence trio (above) split up in 1972, John Fogerty (right) devoted his talents to a solo career.

Teardrops' with his own foot-stomping brand of music. Songs such as 'Almost Saturday Night' and 'Rockin' All Over The World' (a UK Number 3 hit for Status Quo in 1977) were every bit as good as the best of Creedence.

In 1975, there seemed no end to Fogerty's talent and no indication that his creativity and dedication would dry up. But a disillusionment with rock music in general and disputes with his record label, Fantasy, in particular conspired to keep Fogerty out of the public eye for fully a decade.

Then, in a blaze of glory, his 1985 comeback album *Centerfield* on a new label, Warners, shot to Number 1 in the US and spawned a Number 10 single, 'The Old Man Down The Road'. Though the following year's *Eve Of The Zombie* marked time musically, it was good to have Fogerty back recording and touring—and for the first time playing his old Creedence classics solo.　　　　　MAX BELL

CREEDENCE CLEARWATER REVIVAL
Discography

As Tommy Fogerty and the Blue Velvets
Singles
Have You Ever Been Lonely/Bonita (Orchestra 1010, 1964).

As the Golliwogs
Singles
Don't Tell Me No Lies/Little Girl Does Your Mama Know (Fantasy 590, 1965); You Came Walking/Where You Been (Fantasy 597, 1965); You Got Nothin' On Me/You Can't Be True (Fantasy 599, 1965); Brown Eyed Girl/You Better Be Careful (Scorpio 404, 1966); Fight Fire/Fragile Child (Scorpio 405, 1966); Walking On The Water/You Better Get It Before It Gets You (Scorpio 406, 1967); Porterville/Call It Pretending (Scorpio 412, 1967).

As Creedence Clearwater Revival
Singles
Suzie Q. (Part 1)/Suzie Q. (Part 2) (Fantasy 616, 1968); I Put A Spell On You/Walk On The Water (Fantasy 617, 1968); Proud Mary/Born On The Bayou (Fantasy 619, 1969); Bad Moon Rising/Lodi (Fantasy 622, 1969); Green River/Commotion (Fantasy 625, 1969); Down On The Corner/Fortunate Son (Fantasy 634, 1969); Travelin' Band/Who'll Stop The Rain (Fantasy 637, 1970); Up Around The Bend/Run Through The Jungle (Fantasy 641, 1970); Long As I Can See The Light/Lookin' Out My Back Door (Fantasy 645, 1970); Have You Ever Seen The Rain/Hey Tonight (Fantasy 655, 1971); Sweet Hitch Hiker/Door To Door (Fantasy 665, 1971); Someday Never Comes/Tearin' Up The Country (Fantasy 676, 1972); I Heard It Through The Grapevine/Good Golly Miss Molly (Fantasy 759, 1976).

Albums
Creedence Clearwater Revival (Fantasy 8382, 1968); *Bayou Country* (Fantasy 8387, 1969); *Green River* (Fantasy 8393, 1969); *Willy And The Poor Boys* (Fantasy 8397, 1969); *Cosmo's Factory* (Fantasy 8402, 1970); *Pendulum* (Fantasy 8410, 1970); *Mardi Gras* (Fantasy 9404, 1972); *Live In Europe* (Fantasy CCR-1, 1974); *The Golliwogs – Pre-Creedence* (Fantasy 9474, 1975); *The Concert* (Fantasy MPF 4501, 1980).

Rock Around the Maypole

Electric rock recharged traditional British folk in the late Sixties

OPINIONS VARY as to whether British folk-rock began with the release of Davy Graham and Shirley Collins' *Folk Roots, New Routes* in 1964, the Incredible String Band's *5000 Spirits Or The Layers Of The Onion* in 1967, the first Pentangle album in the following year or Fairport Convention's 1969 release, *What We Did On Our Holidays*. Whatever the truth, it is certain that the emergence of a specifically British form of folk-rock music in the late Sixties would not have been possible without the musical ferment of a decade earlier that went by the name of skiffle.

Although skiffle meant simply another musical fashion for the record industry (and one it could promote in the hope of swift profits), at grass-roots level it had provided a new kind of meeting-ground for a whole array of musicians who had previously found no obvious public outlet for their work. The initiators of the skiffle boom had been performers like Lonnie Donegan and Ken Colyer, both members of successful trad jazz bands, but the skiffle clubs also attracted people whose previous musical experience had been in experimental theatre, in radio drama or documentary or simply accompanying obscure records in the privacy of their front rooms. Skiffle also brought together a wide range of musical material. It proved to be the starting-point for two of the most significant trends in British music during the Sixties in the rhythm and blues scene and the music of the folk clubs.

Within the folk-club movement, however,

Richard Thompson plays up to the traditional 'finger-in-the-ear' image of British folk that he, together with fellow members of Fairport Convention, did so much to dispel. Since leaving the band, he continued to work in the folk-rock field, both solo and with wife Linda.

the cheerful eclecticism of the skiffle era was not preserved. It became evident early in the Sixties that the folk scene was divided into two camps. Some clubs became exclusively traditionalist, populated mainly by hand-over-the-ear singers who performed either unaccompanied or with the approved 'traditional' accompaniment of guitar, concertina or fiddle. The 'contemporary' clubs on the other hand featured blues and ragtime instrumentalists as well as singer-songwriters. Each type of club, in its own way, was to make a contribution to the impact of folk on the wider rock arena in the late Sixties.

Solo in Soho

Two of the most renowned contemporary folk clubs were to be found in London – Les Cousins in Soho and the Scots Hoose in Cambridge Circus. The halcyon days of 1963-65 saw them play host to such performers as Paul Simon, Ralph McTell, Davy Graham, Al Stewart, Roy Harper, Donovan, the Young Tradition, Bert Jansch and even, occasionally, Bob Dylan. The most inventive of these fell into two main categories – the 'folk-baroque' guitarists and the singer-songwriters.

The key figure among the first category was Davy Graham. He came to the Soho folk scene having travelled throughout Europe and North Africa, and brought a range of musical influences to match. His repertoire included Irish and English traditional tunes, pieces based on Indian ragas and jazz standards. In playing each piece, he exhibited a style that absorbed and fused together elements from all those traditions. Graham was also one of the first members of the folk scene to land a recording contract. His second album, *Folk Roots, New Routes*, was a collaboration with traditionalist singer Shirley Collins that predated the mingling of approaches that would characterise the later folk-rock work of Sandy Denny with Fairport Convention.

At the time, though, Graham's work was so original that nobody followed its lead fully. But he did inspire a whole group of young guitarists to expand the vocabulary of traditional folk-playing. The most gifted among them were Bert Jansch and John Renbourn. The gaunt Jansch also wrote his own songs and was one of the first 'stars' of the folk circuit. He did not reach beyond the clubs until 1967, however, when he formed the first of the British folk 'crossover' groups, Pentangle, with Renbourn and singer Jacqui McShee. With a jazzy rather than rock-based rhythm section, and using acoustic guitars for the most part, Pentangle became firm favourites on the US and UK college circuits.

Jansch and Renbourn continued their solo careers after Pentangle's demise, but remained on the borderline between the folk world and a larger audience. Pentangle's bassist Danny Thompson went on to accompany a variety of singer/guitarists, including two of the most talented of the contemporary folk-club musicians in John Martyn and Ralph McTell. Martyn could claim to have been a one-man folk-rock movement, since he began to experiment with a range of electronic devices attached to his acoustic guitar that took him towards the rock mainstream.

Electrifying music
Ralph McTell, however, represented the second category of folk performers, being one of the British singer-songwriters to emerge from the Soho scene and establish themselves with concert-hall or rock-club audiences. Like Al Stewart, another folk-club graduate who was later to find success in the United States, McTell established a broad audience that included both folk-song enthusiasts and listeners to what has come to be called 'adult-oriented-rock'. He exemplified folk-rock in the broader sense of the term: music rooted in the folk scene that was developed and performed within the general popular-music context of concert halls, television series and major record companies. A contemporary of McTell's was Roy Harper, whose erratic career comprised work in the narrower sense of 'folk-rock': a specific musical *style* involving the mingling of folk-based songs and tunes with the sound and rhythm of electric instruments played in the rock mode.

Harper was unusual among the performers of folk-rock in this stricter sense in that he came from the contemporary wing of the folk scene. The majority of the folk musicians to embrace a rock idiom in the late Sixties and early Seventies had a traditionalist background. Their reasons for switching from acoustic to electric music were often a mixture of aesthetic, professional and frankly economic motives. Performers like Dave Swarbrick and Tim Hart felt that modern instrumentation

and technology could enhance the dramatic impact of many traditional ballads. 'When you are dealing with, say, violence – someone slashing with a sword,' said Swarbrick, 'there are sounds which exist electrically – with electric bass, say – that can very explicitly suggest what the words are saying.' Tim Hart's defence of folk-rock was to argue that rock instruments were as valid an accompaniment to folk songs as the acoustic guitars favoured by the folk purists: 'Most English song is unaccompanied song, and the only argument is – should you or should you not accompany it at all?'

Both Hart and Swarbrick (who were to become the mainstays of Steeleye Span and Fairport Convention respectively) also felt the restrictions of the folk scene. There was an exclusive, cultist feeling among many of those in charge that sought to preserve folk music from outsiders who might dilute it, thereby imposing a limitation on the size of audience the stars of the circuit might reach. Entrance to folk clubs in the Sixties cost only a few shillings and most clubs could hold less than 100 people, so the financial rewards and public recognition for even the most popular performers were relatively small.

Breaking the mould
When the break into folk-rock came, it was through a group whose members had few folk roots at all. Fairport Convention was made up mainly of musicians inspired by the example of US groups like Jefferson Airplane and a liking for the songs of such writers as Joni Mitchell and Leonard Cohen. In 1967 they launched themselves into the growing London club scene, playing alongside the likes of Pink Floyd and the Incredible String Band. The latter was a group from the Glasgow folk scene with a Davy Graham-like range of musical influences and a selection of songs that mingled the direct imagery of the folk tradition with a vague spirituality in keeping with the hippie mood of the times.

Fairport turned to British folk-rock through vocalist Sandy Denny who joined in 1968, bringing with her a repertoire of traditional ballads from the folk clubs. Rock arrangements of these featuring the original guitar-style of Richard Thompson soon became the keystone of the band's repertoire. Other bands followed suit: Steeleye Span was formed in 1969, and the first of Ashley Hutchings' various Albion Bands in 1972. Steeleye and Fairport were to remain by far the two most successful folk-rock bands during the Seventies, despite the fact that both were afflicted by frequent personnel changes, with the departing members often founding (usually short-lived) rival groups.

Many bands sprang up in the folk-rock field in the Seventies, but most found it difficult to survive for any length of time. Scotland supplied the JSD Band, Newcastle offered Lindisfarne, later Jack the Lad and Hedgehog Pie (who only kept going by switching back from an electric to an acoustic line-up), while the Amazing Blondel, Planxty, Mr Fox, Decameron and the Dransfields appeared elsewhere. All had many valid musical ideas, but without exception were eventually defeated by their position in a no-man's-land between the introverted folk world and the increasingly

Inset below: Singer-songwriter Ralph McTell joins Dave Swarbrick on stage at a Fairport Convention reunion concert in 1979. Bottom: Newcastle's Lindisfarne found success with their particular brand of Geordie folk-rock.

conservative rock scene, where promoters and recording executives were suspicious of new ideas. Eventually the sheer cost of keeping an electric group on the road took its toll.

The folk-rock exemplified by Steeleye Span and Fairport Convention died sometime in the late Seventies, but the notion of a merging of the energies of folk music and rock still re-tained its potency. In 1982, Kevin Rowland's Dexy's Midnight Runners boldly experimented in fusing folk with white soul, scoring a Number 1 hit with 'Come On Eileen', while a succession of singers and bands have come up with the odd folk-influenced single whose novelty has caught the public's imagination.

DAVE LAING

Inset below left: Al Stewart, a graduate of the folk circuit who found commercial success in the States during the Seventies. Inset below: 'Folk-baroque' guitarist Davy Graham was one of the first British folkies to secure a recording contract.

FAIRPORT'S FULL HOUSE

The Convention that became an institution

IF MUSICAL INFLUENCE were rewarded with ready money, Fairport Convention would have been a very rich group indeed. Talking of 'Fairport Convention' is never quite that simple, however: they were never just one band. During their official 12-year existence, Fairport recorded nearly 20 albums, saw over 20 musicians through the ranks and were responsible for nurturing the careers of some of Britain's finest rock talents. Without Fairport, there would have been no Steeleye Span, Matthews Southern Comfort, Plainsong, Fotheringay, Richard and Linda Thompson, Albion Band, Home Service or, probably, Moving Hearts. Fairport were genuinely inspirational, setting an example for a generation of British bands. Their fusion of traditional folk and rock infuriated purists, but made many rock fans aware of Britain's folk tradition.

Fairport were quick to attain a legendary status after their formation. By the end of the Sixties it seemed they had always been there – an ever-changing band of folk gypsies playing an intoxicating brew of skirling ethnic melodies, golden ballads and driving rock. They perfected the electric-folk form both live and on record, at their very best when led by the furious fiddling of Dave Swarbrick and the lustrous vocals of Sandy Denny. What Fairport most memorably brought to folk was a dynamic electric tension: masterpieces like 'Matty Groves', 'Sloth' and 'Hanging Song' crackle with drama, emotion and a sense of fatefulness. This same power also supercharges the band's jigs and reels.

Muswell hillbillies

The seeds of Fairport Convention were sown in the North London suburb of Muswell Hill by Ashley Hutchings, a skiffle and Radio Luxembourg fan and bass player, who formed a series of blues and country-based bands in the mid Sixties, among them the Electric Dysentery and the Ethnic Shuffle Orchestra. With rhythm guitarist Simon Nicol, drummer Martin Lamble and the precociously talented Richard Thompson on lead guitar joining Hutchings, Fairport Convention began to take shape in early 1967.

The group took their name from Simon Nicol's house, and once together played the usual round of church halls and friends' parties with a repertoire that was heavily American-influenced – including songs by Bob Dylan, Richard Farina, Phil Ochs and Jefferson Airplane. But Fairport were light on the vocal front, so two singers, Judy Dyble and former Bradford City footballer Ian Matthews, were invited to join.

Pioneering American record-producer and London underground figure Joe Boyd spotted the six-piece group at a London psychedelic club, Happening 44, and – fascinated by 17-year-old Richard Thompson's fluid guitar style – offered them work on the busy underground circuit, notably at UFO, which he ran, and Middle Earth. He also secured them a recording deal with Track Records: the first Fairport Convention single was a Thirties jazz song, 'If I Had A Ribbon Bow', which sank unnoticed. Their debut album was recorded for Polydor, and included songs by the then-unknown Joni Mitchell, and a rare Dylan song, 'Jack O'Diamonds', alongside the band's own material.

Sandy on holiday

Following Judy Dyble's departure to Giles, Giles and Fripp, Fairport recruited Sandy Denny in May 1968. Sandy had attended Kingston Art College and, while working as a nurse, had begun singing solo around the London folk clubs, later joining an early line-up of the Strawbs. With Sandy's influence – and her full, effulgent voice to the fore – the band began to tap the rich seam of traditional folk music and entered their most artistically successful period. A shimmering version of the traditional 'Nottamun Town' on 1969's What We Did On Our Holidays indicated the new direction. It was a confident debut on the Island label – the album radiated delicacy, and introduced such Fairport favourites as

Inset opposite: Fairport convene in 1968 – from left Martin Lamble, Simon Nicol, Judy Dyble, Richard Thompson, Ian Matthews and Ashley Hutchings. Opposite: Sandy Denny. Above: 1969 Convention with Sandy and new boys Dave Swarbrick (in sandals) and Dave Mattacks (in sunglasses).

'Fotheringay' and 'Meet On The Ledge'.

Fairport Convention were not the first group to tackle sacrosanct folk music in a fresh way – Pentangle and Sweeney's Men had already issued their imaginative debut albums. But when Fairport recorded their interpretation of 'A Sailor's Life' on their third album, Unhalfbricking (1969), both they and producer Boyd realised what a landmark it was. One of the best-known traditional songs, it was transformed into a seething electric jam, a masterful combination of folk, rock and jazz. 'A Sailor's Life' also featured the traditional folk world's best-known fiddler, Dave Swarbrick. Swarb's reputation in the folk scene was impeccable – he was especially renowned for his work with the Ian Campbell Folk Group and Martin Carthy.

Swarbrick's arrival brought a vast knowledge of traditional music into the band, but his whole-hearted embracing of Fairport's iconoclastic 'folk-rock' upset the traditionalists. With that third album, Fairport also demonstrated they had two brilliant 'in-house' writers in Sandy Denny, who contributed her finest song, the haunting, autumnal 'Who Knows Where The Time Goes', and Richard Thompson, whose contributions included the atmospheric 'Genesis Hall'. Also on the LP was 'Si Tu Dois Partir', a rousing version of Dylan's 'If You Gotta Go', which gave Fairport their only hit single when it reached Number 21 in the UK Top Thirty in July 1969.

Ian Matthews, unhappy with the band's growing emphasis on electric-folk, had left during the recording of Unhalfbricking. He went on to form the country-influenced Matthews Southern Comfort immediately after leaving Fairport, and had a UK Number 1 single in 1970 with Joni Mitchell's 'Woodstock'. Matthews later formed Plainsong and afterwards went solo.

Liege lords

Returning from a gig in Birmingham in June 1969, Fairport were involved in a motorway smash and drummer Martin Lamble was killed. The tragedy marked a turning-point for the band. After deciding to carry on, Fairport called in drummer Dave Mattacks, confirmed Dave Swarbrick as a permanent member, and went on to record British folk-rock's crucial album. Liege And Lief was released in December 1969, and brought Fairport's experiments in electric-folk to magnificent fruition. By applying the immediacy and technology of rock to a traditional ballad like 'Matty Groves', Fairport found themselves in the vanguard of an exciting new movement.

While folk artists like Davy Graham and Shirley Collins had approached traditional music from a strictly non-traditional angle, Fairport were the first rock band to do so. Their urgent electric music accentuated the powerful rhythms the traditional songs contained, and yet opened up the rich legacy of traditional folk to a vast young audience. Richard Thompson and Dave Swarbrick, in a fruitful but short-lived partnership, collaborated on songs strongly in the traditional idiom, as the sad and gentle 'Crazy Man Michael' from Liege And Lief and the beautifully restrained 'Sloth' from Full House (1970) testify.

Just when the time seemed right for Fairport to capitalise on the innovatory *Liege And Lief*, the group was split down the middle. Ashley Hutchings, founder-member, bass-player and prime mover behind the switch to electric-folk, left the band. He wished to explore the possibilities of folk-rock in a more traditional vein and went on to form Steeleye Span with Gay and Terry Woods. Meanwhile, Sandy Denny saw Fairport irrevocably bound to traditional compositions, which she saw as an inevitable limitation on her own writing, and left to start Fotheringay.

The band decided to press on and swiftly engaged bassist Dave Pegg, formerly with various Birmingham R&B bands and an old pal of Swarbrick in the Ian Campbell Folk Group. Finding a singer proved more of a problem; contractually committed to recording another album, the five remaining members – Thompson, Nicol, Mattacks, Swarbrick and Pegg – went into the studio without a recognised vocalist to cut one of their best albums, *Full House*.

Early in 1971, guitarist Richard Thompson quit the band to pursue a solo career. His post-Fairport career has been sporadic, but richly rewarding, yielding such fine solo albums as *Henry The Human Fly* (1972), and six with his wife Linda, notably *I Want To See The Bright Lights Tonight* (1974) and *Shoot Out The Lights* (1982).

June delight
Thompson's departure from Fairport saw the band enter their most confused period. Simon Nicol switched to lead guitar in Thompson's wake, and admitted it was like 'trying to be Hank Marvin *and* Bruce Welch'. In June 1971 the new slim-line four-piece Fairport released *Angel Delight*. The album blended new and traditional material in the same successful formula as *Full House*, and demonstrated Swarbrick's growing facility as an artful-voiced singer – particularly on the comic Fairport autobiography of 'Angel Delight' itself, and on the bawdy 'Bonny Black Hare'. It was Swarbrick's energy, too, that saw through the *Babbacombe Lee* concept album, released that November. The true story of John 'Babbacombe' Lee – a convicted murderer who cheated the hangman three

times – provided Fairport with the ideal narrative for some of their most dramatic songs, notably 'Hanging Song'.

Upset by the group's criticism of his production of the album, Simon Nicol – the last original member of Fairport Convention – quit at the end of 1971. It was to be 18 months before Fairport released another album. A fluctuating series of line-ups fol-

lowed, and even Fairport's most devout fans felt the group could not carry on. It took the arrival of Trevor Lucas and American-born Jerry Donahue from Sandy Denny's defunct Fotheringay (plus the return of drummer Dave Mattacks) to give Fairport the creative shot in the arm they sorely needed.

The new line-up found its feet in 1973 with the patchy *Rosie* album, following this with a classic in *Fairport Convention Nine*. The latter saw Fairport again imaginatively tackling traditional folk material (for example 'Polly On The Shore'), but also incorporating songs influenced by country and western music. Lucas was by now married to Sandy Denny and in March 1974 Fairport's most famous singer rejoined the group herself.

This new line-up undertook a successful world tour, and recorded the impressive *Rising For The Moon* album in 1974. It looked as though Fairport Convention were set to become a major force again, but the album's release preceded the departure of Sandy, Trevor and Dave Mattacks.

Despite being voted Britain's Best Female Singer for two consecutive years in

the *Melody Maker* poll, Sandy Denny never attained the success of her North American singer-songwriter contemporaries, though Judy Collins' version of 'Who Knows Where The Time Goes' testified to her influence. Sandy proved her talent as early as the charming album she recorded with the Strawbs in 1967, allowed it to blossom during her first stint with Fairport and let it grow to full maturity with her group Fotheringay and on her four solo albums. Those albums (notably 1971's *The North Star Grassman And The Raven*) demonstrated her broad musical knowledge as well as her own writing skill – and, of course, that crystal-clear voice.

Between her stays with Fairport, Sandy took time off from her solo career to duet with Robert Plant on 'The Battle of Evermore' on the fourth Led Zeppelin album (1971), took part in Lou Reizner's 1972 production of the Who's rock-opera *Tommy* and recorded an album of rock'n'roll standards with the Bunch in 1972. Her tragic death from a brain haemorrhage (following a fall) at the age of 31 in 1978 robbed British rock music of one of its most precious talents.

Fairport's changing faces. Below: The class of '71 – from left Nicol (who switched to lead guitar after Thompson's departure), Mattacks, Swarbrick and Dave Pegg. Opposite: On television in 1973 with Trevor Lucas (left) and Jerry Donahue (centre). Above: A 1975 appearance with Sandy Denny back in the fold and Swarbrick at full throttle.

Time, gentlemen, please

Former Grease Band drummer Bruce Rowland had joined Fairport (which very briefly became the band's name), and with an enlarged line-up (including the Breton Dan Ar Bras, Alan Stivell's guitarist) they recorded their last album for Island, the disastrous *Gottle O'Geer* (1976). This version of Fairport was short-lived, too, and with founder member Simon Nicol rejoining the nucleus of Swarbrick, Pegg and Rowland, and a new record deal with Vertigo, Fairport Convention continued their remarkable saga with an unexpectedly fine album in 1977 – *The Bonny Bunch Of Roses*, notable for its epic title track and the economy of the band's playing. Strong as that album was, it proved to be a flash in the pan, and after two further desultory albums, *Tipplers Tales* (1978) and *Farewell Farewell* (1979), Fairport called it a day in the summer of 1979.

Dave Pegg went straight into Jethro Tull; Simon Nicol and Dave Swarbrick continued to perform acoustically around the folk clubs; Bruce Rowland was kept busy with sessions, while Dave Mattacks played on Paul McCartney's 1982 album *Tug Of War*. But ties proved strong, and a 1980 reunion gig became an annual event. A Pegg and Mattacks-led line-up has also recorded and toured sporadically.

Fairport Convention will be remembered for a lot more than cosy nostalgia, however. They were the first band to demonstrate the possibilities of marrying rock'n'roll rhythms to traditional folk material. From Fairport's initial fusion, the band developed its own identity. And from under that Fairport umbrella came talents like Sandy Denny, Richard Thompson and Ashley Hutchings. The group's legacy is the rich mine of electric folk-rock they opened up. The rest, as they say, is history.   PATRICK HUMPHRIES

**Fairport Convention
Recommended Listening**

The History Of Fairport Convention (Island ICD 4) (Includes: Meet On The Ledge, Sailor's Life, Sloth, Matty Groves, Who Knows Where The Time Goes, Hanging Song, Fotheringay).

THE INCREDIBLES' JOURNEY

Trailblazing sounds from the Incredible String Band

THE PRICE TO PAY for being a part of your time is that you may not fit into any other. Some old pop music appeals because it is timeless and some because it is indelibly stamped with the mark of its era. Along with Donovan and George Harrison, the Incredible String Band summed up for many people what life was all about in the late Sixties.

Clive's Incredible String Band, as the outfit was originally known, was formed in Edinburgh in 1965 by Clive Palmer (banjo, guitar and vocals) and Robin Williamson (violin, guitar and vocals). After playing

around the then-burgeoning folk club circuit in and around Edinburgh, the duo was joined at the end of the year by guitarist and singer Mike Heron. The 'Clive' prefix was dropped and the Incredible String Band was born.

Mad hatters

The folk scene in 1965 was a lot closer to Tin Pan Alley than it is today. Though their music was far from traditional, Donovan, Bob Dylan, and Joan Baez had all made the Top Twenty with just their acoustic guitars for backing: and the hypnotic nasal drone that broadly typified folk-rock vocals found echoes in the fully-fledged pop music of the Beatles, the Byrds

and Sonny and Cher. It was thus possible for three Scotsmen virtually unknown outside their home town to secure a long-term album deal with Elektra, itself fast developing a reputation as a 'progressive' international label.

The first LP, simply entitled *The Incredible String Band*, was recorded in one afternoon at Sound Techniques in Chelsea and released in mid 1966. In comparison to what was to come, it was a simple record; there were no overdubs and fairly simple lyrics. But what was immediately impressive was the degree to which these unknowns had developed such a unique, personal and intricate way of songwriting – or, at least, two of them had. The bulk of

the material was divided between Heron and Williamson, with Clive Palmer contributing only one song and a banjo instrumental. Ousted by the exploding creativity of the others, Palmer took his share of the recording advance and disappeared south.

What remained was to be the Incredible String Band at its best. 'Band' seemed an exaggerated way to describe only two musicians, but, with the aid of newly-developed techniques of multi-tracking, they soon created a sort of humming, buzzing, crawling sound that at times resembled a hive set to music, at other times a choir of lost souls moaning in a long-abandoned Highland fortress. Heron and Williamson could make two musicians sound like twenty.

With Palmer gone, it was at once apparent how complementary the remaining duo were. Mike Heron songs like 'Painting Box', 'The Hedgehog's Song' and 'Little Cloud' were catchy and accessible in a way that perfectly offset the exotic and sinuous meanderings of Williamson. And it was on the second album, *The 5000 Spirits Or The Layers Of The Onion* (1967), that the typical Incredible String Band sound first appeared, particularly on 'The Mad Hatter's Song' where sitar, double-bass and piano all featured by turns as Robin Williamson strung together ten tunes in five minutes.

The *5000 Spirits* remains to this day eerie, remote, wistful,

humorous and exciting. As with the follow-up LP – *The Hangman's Beautiful Daughter*, released in March 1968 – the prime feeling was one of expectancy, a feeling that there is more to life than meets the eye, that every physical thing harbours a spirit of some sort. The music of the Incredible String Band depicted a clear-cut lifestyle, one of living in the country, vegetarianism, Scientology, concern for all living things as well as a hefty slice of hippie indulgence.

By this stage, the duo had become celebrated multi-instrumentalists; Heron restricted himself to guitar, sitar and keyboards but Williamson managed to play gimbri (a kind of mournful Arab fiddle), mandolin, Jew's harp, whistle, harmonica and drums as well. They had acquired an intensely devoted following, who helped *The Hangman's Beautiful Daughter* to reach Number 7 in the UK album charts, and in mid 1968 the underground paper *International Times* commented: 'The Incredible String Band can only become more incredible.' But the paper had got it wrong. For – like many wayward talents – what made the duo great was also their undoing. Aided by their scriptures, their drugs and their faithful following, Heron

Opposite: The Incredible String Band exude a festive spirit on stage. Below: Mike Heron (left) and Robin Williamson with girlfriends Rose and Licorice and an assortment of exotic instruments.

and Williamson had created an innocent, childlike world of their own. That they were sincere is beyond doubt, and such was their sincerity that they eventually abandoned drugs and embraced Scientology as a means of fixing a permanent smile on their faces where grass had given them only a temporary one.

At this turning point they recorded their last great LP, a double album called *Wee Tam And The Big Huge*, which was released in the autumn of 1968. Their personalities had drifted nearer the surface but further away from each other, and by this stage they were accompanied on much of the material by their girlfriends Rose Simpson and Licorice McKechnie. While the girls may have enhanced the atmosphere at gigs, they contributed little to the albums that could not have been achieved by either Mike or Robin doing overdubs. The girls seemed there mainly for the purpose of keeping Heron and

Williamson together by acting as a buffer between them.

Despite this, *Wee Tam* contained some of their best performances to date. Like a field in high summer, when the nights have already begun to draw back in, the music had reached the extent of its growth but still exuded a golden warmth. Mike Heron came up with the vintage singalong 'Cousin Caterpillar' and contributed some languid, jangling sitar to Robin Williamson's epic tales of mankind ('Maya') and lost time redeemed ('The Iron Stone'). 'The Yellow Snake', also with the classic guitar/sitar sound, was a timeless celebration of being, while on 'Douglas Traherne Harding' Mike sang an uncharacteristically

Below: Way back in the Sixties – Heron and Williamson harmonise and gather woodfolk for the cover of The Hangman's Beautiful Daughter *(inset left). Inset right: 1968's* Wee Tam *– their last great album.*

long and rambling story about a man who has no head, one eye, a body filled with light and lives in a basement.

But by their next album, *Changing Horses*, a year later, the rot had set in and the spell was broken. Time had started to flow again and the band was trying to move with it: but whereas previously they had kept abreast of time, their incorporation of electric guitar, bass and drums ensured that they were now well behind it. Where they had sounded proficient, if a little stoned, on acoustic instruments, they sounded lost and amateurish on amplified ones. This was one area where Heron was a lot more at home than Williamson, with the result that, instead of complementing each other, they started to sound inappropriate on each other's tracks.

Silken dreams

The ISB's other problem was how to keep saying the same thing over and over and still make it sound fresh. The fixed grins seemed more hollow, the songs of praise less heartfelt and more obligatory, until the only great moments came when the masks slipped and the men behind the grins were allowed to sing out. Most of these moments came from Robin Williamson, after he had trimmed his epics, trimmed his hair, and valiantly struggled into early Seventies Kings Road gear to try and 'communicate' with the so-called real world. 1972 produced the dismal *Earthspan* LP, which featured bass-player/vocalist Malcolm LeMaistre, who tried to write old-style String Band songs because neither Mike nor Robin could be bothered.

Although their records were losing their colour, the band was still popular live. Rose and Licorice had made way for LeMaistre and a host of Scientologist session men, but Williamson and Heron somehow still charmed the audiences into the halls. They hardly played on each other's songs anymore, however – the exception being two beautiful tracks on their final LP, *Hard Rope And Silken Twine* (1974), both written by Williamson. 'Cold February' could have passed for an old Irish hymn, but was a deeply moving antiwar song, while 'Dreams Of No Return' featured for one final time the ecstatic blend of Mike's sitar and Robin's guitar, with no hamfisted concessions to rock 'n'roll.

The Incredible String Band finally split in November 1974, with Robin flying to California to immerse himself in various folk-music projects, and Mike forming several rock acts around the remains of the Incredibles. Sadly, what might have seemed progressive in the early Seventies, when Heron first manifested his hard-rock tendencies, seemed pointless and dated by the middle of the decade. Robin Williamson, meanwhile, showed on his solo LP releases that he was as stuck in folk as Heron was in rock, but these later deficiencies only served to highlight the early brilliance of the aptly-named Incredible String Band.
LUTHER PAISLEY

Incredible String Band Recommended Listening

The 5000 Spirits Or The Layers Of The Onion (Elektra K 42001) (Includes: Chinese White, No Sleep Blues, Painting Box, The Mad Hatter's Song, The Eyes Of Fate, The Hedgehog's Song, Way Back In The 1960s); *The Hangman's Beautiful Daughter* (Elektra K 42002) (Includes: Witches Hat, A Very Cellular Song, Mercy I Cry City, The Water Song, Three Is A Green Crown, Nightfall).

STEELEYE SPAN

The band that brought flamboyance to folk-rock

JOHN 'STEELEYE' SPAN was a waggoner on a North Lincolnshire farm in the early nine-teenth century. He was immortalised in a song called 'Horkstow Grange', which described a fight between him and a labourer called John Bowlin. The song was brought to the English folk revival by the collector Percy Grainger, and caught the imagination of a club singer called Tim Hart. In 1969, when Tim found himself involved in choosing a name for an electric folk group, Steeleye Span came to mind.

At that time, the folk-rock music of Fair-port Convention had still not reached a mass audience, but it had done enough to split the tightly-knit world of folk wide open. Did their controversial treatment of the British folk legacy mean its ultimate

Right: Original Steeleye – from left Ashley Hutchings, Gay and Terry Woods, Maddy Prior and Tim Hart. Below: Spanning the beach, 1978.

destruction, or was it an authentic development? At the time this question was being asked, Tim Hart and his partner Maddy Prior had outgrown the folk-club circuit and were looking for a new challenge. In the summer of 1969 they met up with former Fairport Convention member Ashley Hutchings and two Irish musicians, Gay and Terry Woods, all of whom wanted to explore electric folk.

Hutchings was convinced that Fairport Convention had not been faithful enough to the British folk-song repertoire, and that there was a need for a band who could produce rock arrangements of the original words and melodies of the folk tradition. So the five formed Steeleye Span, and in March 1970 they spent a week in the studio recording *Hark! The Village Wait*, their first album for RCA.

The album included Hutchings' electric bass and a range of stringed instruments from guitars to mandolin, but no drums. The songs were drawn from the traditional repertoires of England, Scotland and Ireland, and featured outstanding vocal duets by Gay Woods and Maddy Prior. Before the album was released, however, Steeleye Span suffered their first of many personnel changes when the Woods' left the band to return to Ireland.

Two turn up

Steeleye's first live concert was thus postponed until September 1970, by which time the line-up included two new members in guitarist Martin Carthy and fiddler Peter Knight. Carthy was already a highly respected folk musician, renowned for having tutored both Bob Dylan and Paul Simon in English folk songs. He had previously been part of an acoustic duo with violinist Dave Swarbrick, until Swarbrick had gone electric and joined Fairport Convention. Peter Knight, on the other hand, was an assistant in a London music shop and completely unknown.

Neither of the new members had played electric music before, and at first it showed. In live performances they tended to play at maximum volume. Fortunately, this was not the case on the line-up's first album together. Released in March 1971, *Please To See The King* remains one of the most original-sounding electric-folk experiments of the period, mainly because Martin Carthy had not grown up with a background in rock music. This was an advantage, as the range of amplified sounds on guitars, banjo and mandolin could be moulded to the contours of the folk melodies, rather than the melodies being subservient to the rock rhythm.

During 1971, Steeleye Span began to build up a reputation within the growing folk-rock movement in Britain, touring first with Jethro Tull and then headlining their own month-long tour. But the year ended with the departure of yet more members: Ashley Hutchings left to pursue his own ideas about English electric folk, while Martin Carthy returned to the folk-club scene.

Stars in the making

This was a turning-point for the band, both musically and as a commercial proposition. They began to veer away from purist folk and seek an international reputation. Their musical direction for the next four years was set by the addition of two players with a strong rock background: Bob Johnson on guitar and bassist Rick Kemp, formerly with Michael Chapman. On the business side, Steeleye replaced their manager and record producer Sandy Roberton with Jo Lustig, an ebullient New Yorker who persuaded the band that he could make them worldwide stars.

Lustig's scheme was to apply to Steeleye the strategy that had made earlier British bands like Procol Harum and Jethro Tull global successes. This involved exhaustingly lengthy US tours, greater visual impact in live performance and regular album production. Between 1972 and 1976, the band went to the States four

times and Australia twice, producing six studio albums along the way.

The Steeleye sound became heavier, shifting from the electric folk of the previous period to a folk-rock sound with a balanced mix of each type of music. Bob Johnson was in many ways a conventional rock guitarist (he had worked as a session man with P. J. Proby among others) and his strongly chorded style was well suited to some of the more melodramatic traditional lyrics that became Steeleye trademarks. These included 'Long Lankin' (recorded on the 1975 album *Commoner's Crown*), 'Thomas The Rhymer' and 'Seven Hundred Elves' (both from the previous year's *Now We Are Six*).

The title of this last album referred not only to its position as the band's sixth LP, but to a new member of the band. The addition of ex-Gnidrolog drummer Nigel Pegrum underlined the growing commitment to rock rhythms. *Now We Are Six* was

recorded soundtrack. The play was taken to America and Australia in 1974.

Despite all the touring and the well-received albums, Steeleye never quite broke though to international star status. New manager Tony Secunda resorted to a variety of gimmicks to promote the band. In Australia he caused an uproar by offering '12 hours with a member of the band' as a competition prize, while the audience at a London concert in October 1976 were amazed to find pound notes floating down from the roof during an encore.

Storms and splits

At the start of 1977, Steeleye Span announced they were to stop work for six months. Even if Lustig's international strategy had not worked, they were solidly established within the UK, with two Top Ten singles behind them: the acappella 'Gaudete' (1973) and the strongly rhythmic 'All Around My Hat' (1975). The latter had been produced by Wombles mastermind Mike Batt, and its unashamedly pop format surprised many observers. But Bob Johnson and Peter Knight had begun work on an album called *The King Of Elfland's Daughter*, and in May 1977 they announced that they were to leave the band.

The four remaining members decided to continue for another album and British tour and brought back Martin Carthy and concertina virtuoso John Kirkpatrick to record the tenth Steeleye album, *Storm Force Ten*. The 'final UK tour' took place in March 1978, after which Tim Hart and Maddy Prior departed to pursue solo careers, while Nigel Pegrum devoted himself to his Plant Life folk record label. Rick Kemp took part in a number of projects as performer or producer and married Maddy Prior. But the individual musicians were to find that the reputation of Steeleye and the pressures to re-form were enormous.

A new album, *Sails Of Silver*, duly appeared in 1980 and the most successful Steeleye line-up (including Johnson, Kemp and Pegrum) again took to the road, undertaking a lengthy British tour and going on to headline 1981's Cambridge Folk Festival. *Back In Line* (1986) was the belated follow-up, though more praise was reserved for *No More To The Dance* Prior's 1988 repeat of her 1976 *Silly Sisters* collaboration with June Tabor.

Steeleye's place in music history, however, is assured. Between 1972 and 1976 they were the group that most extensively and logically explored the folk-rock formula: they put in practice the theory that the way to make traditional songs into contemporary ones was to detach them from their original settings and unite them with the sounds and rhythms of modern mainstream rock.   DAVE LAING

Top: The group perform their medieval mummers' play in 1974. Above: On stage in more familiar garb.

produced by Jethro Tull's Ian Anderson and featured a cameo appearance by David Bowie on saxophone.

The melodrama of the lyrics was matched by a more dramatic approach to stage performance. During 1971 and 1972 Steeleye had performed in historical plays written by Keith Dewhurst for theatres in London and Edinburgh, and these inspired Tim Hart to write a version of a medieval mummers' play for presentation as part of the Steeleye stage act. For this the band appeared in traditional costumes, wearing masks and miming their lines to a pre-

ROCK ON THE TYNE

Newcastle folk with Alan Hull and Lindisfarne

LINDISFARNE were rabble-rousers for Tyneside youth for a couple of years in the early Seventies. Each of their memorable concerts was a slice of local life: the band's chugging, ribald folk-rock became the favoured sound of an always enthusiastic audience whose other passions were the local beer and Newcastle football club. They toured successfully throughout Britain, of course, but it was always on their home ground that they performed their music best—and not just the boozy, uptempo numbers. The fragile beauty of a song like 'Lady Eleanor', played live, showed the more contemplative side of Lindisfarne.

Lindisfarne's original line-up were together under that name for just three years, and after the band split up, none of its five members was to enjoy comparable success. The nucleus of the band came together in Newcastle during the mid Sixties. Ray Laidlaw (drums) and Ray Jackson (harmonica, mandolin) were art students, Simon Cowe (guitar) worked in a city-centre photographic store and Rod Clements (bass) was a student at Durham University.

'In the famous summer of 1967,' recalled Clements, 'we were the Downtown Faction, one of the underground bands in Newcastle, playing at places like the Key Club and the Club A Go Go, which the Animals wrote a song about. We also used to play at dances down at the coast in the summer and all the freaks came.' At this time, the band had two acts: an electric bluesy 'underground' set for the dances, and one with acoustic instruments, featuring their own compositions, for the folk clubs.

In 1968, the band, renamed the Brethren, met up with Alan Hull – a prolific local singer-songwriter and an established figure on the north-east folk club circuit. He had previously been in a Newcastle band called the Chosen Few who were contemporaries of the Animals and had cut a few singles in the mid Sixties. Initially, the Brethren backed Hull on some demonstration discs cut at a local studio, and these tracks were later released on a Rubber Records sampler called *Take Off Your Head And Listen*. Among them was 'We Can Swing Together', a number that became a Lindisfarne sing-along standard. Its constant revival, though, indicated one of the band's weaknesses – they were never able to produce a sufficient quantity of new material to match the old favourites.

Alan Hull and the Brethren then joined forces on a permanent basis and were signed to a recording contract by Tony

Stratton-Smith, boss of the independent Charisma label. The name Lindisfarne – that of a Northumbrian island famous for its history and seventh-century Gospels – was chosen shortly before the release of the first LP, *Nicely Out Of Tune* (1970). Although both the playing and the production were more ragged than on subsequent recordings, the essential character of the band came through loud and clear. The album revealed Alan Hull's songwriting skills in the combination of lush romanticism employed on 'Lady Eleanor' and 'Clear White Light', with the earthy humour of 'We Can Swing Together', the raucous tale of a run-in with the forces of the law.

Dead-end ditties

Nicely Out Of Tune received polite rather than ecstatic reviews, and for the next Lindisfarne album Stratton-Smith brought in Bob Johnston, the renowned American producer of Bob Dylan and others. According to Rod Clements, the sound on *Fog On The Tyne* (1971) was very much Johnston's idea, and the crisper, neater sound paid off for the band. Early in 1972 they had their first hit single from the album when the Dylanesque 'Meet Me On The Corner', featuring Jackson's harmonica-playing, reached Number 5 in the UK. At the same time the album sales soared, and the LP spent 21 weeks in the Top Ten. Charisma then re-issued the earlier unsuccessful 'Lady Eleanor', which this time reached Number 3.

Although it was not intended to be a 'concept' album, the compositions on *Fog On The Tyne* were to be regarded as a set of songs, taking the theme of the young unemployed in a provincial city making what they could of a situation full of dead-ends. The title song treated the subject with both humour and irony, outlining the possibilities available to kids with too much time on their hands and too little money. The album's title track soon became the climax of Lindisfarne's live appearances in concert halls and at festivals in 1971 and 1972.

The audience participation engendered by Lindisfarne at their gigs was remarkable. But that participation, and the expectations that the band would provide more such anthems, contributed to the failure of the third album *Dingly Dell* (1972).

By this time the band was under some strain. Two American tours had failed to reproduce their British success, and Alan Hull was finding it hard to produce enough new songs for recording. Several of the tracks on *Dingly Dell* were old numbers, and the title piece was a pretentious flop. In May 1973, Lindisfarne split in two with Alan Hull and Ray Jackson retaining the name while the other three formed a new band, Jack the Lad, who developed an engaging brand of folk-rock over a series of albums in the mid Seventies, but never managed to break out of the club circuit in the way the old Lindisfarne had.

The new Lindisfarne had little success either. Hull and Jackson recruited four more Newcastle musicians – Kenny Craddock (keyboards), Charlie Harcourt (guitar), Tommy Duffy (bass) and Paul Nichols (drums) – and cut two further albums before the group disbanded in 1975. Alan Hull had also been pursuing an erratic solo career on record, his best album being the caustic *Pipedream* (1973).

None of the original Lindisfarne members were able to find a suitable and popular format for their subsequent work, and a re-formation of Lindisfarne seemed on the cards. The band were tempted into it at Christmas 1976, following this up with a succession of annual reunion gigs. And, although they recorded some new material, scoring a hit with 'Run For Home' in 1978, it was still their trusty old anthems that their audiences flocked to hear.

DAVE LAING

Lindisfarne
Recommended Listening

Lindisfarne's Finest Hour (Charisma CAS 1108) (Includes: Lady Eleanor, Meet Me On The Corner, Down, Scarecrow Song, Fog On The Tyne, Go Back, Alan In The River With Flowers).

Right: The original Lindisfarne, from left Ray Jackson, Alan Hull, Ray Laidlaw, Simon Cowe and Rod Clements. Inset left: The new line-up on stage, 1974. Opposite: Hull maintains the band's boozy image.

FIVE-STAR FOLK

Did Pentangle shape a new musical blend?

PENTANGLE HAVE slipped so far back in the memory of most Sixties rock fans that it is difficult to recall how popular they were at the close of the decade. At that time the group could fill London's Royal Albert Hall without difficulty (as the cover picture of their *Basket Of Light* album suggested), and they were an international attraction of some standing. They were also in the premier rank of groups playing the UK concert hall and college circuit, on a par with such rock acts as Traffic, Pink Floyd and the Who. The fact that this seemed unimaginable a decade later is probably explained by the subsequent total eclipse of commercial folk music.

Pentangle was formed around the twin talents of guitarists Bert Jansch and John Renbourn. Both were prime exponents of the so-called folk baroque, a tradition instigated just a few years earlier by Davy Graham that had brought an instrumental virtuosity and eclecticism to folk for the first time. Jansch, born in Edinburgh on 3 November 1943 of Scottish-Austrian parentage, had become famous in folk clubs – a brooding, uncommunicative performer who found celebrity with songs like Graham's 'Anji' and his own 'Needle of Death'. (He subsequently disowned the latter, though at the time it was one of the most forthright and chilling songs about heroin addiction.) Both Jansch and Renbourn, a native Londoner, were influenced by American bluesmen like Big Bill Broonzy, although Jansch was the one who used such influences to fire his own songwriting technique; Renbourn subsequently developed an interest in the roots of English music.

The folk clubs of the mid Sixties were booming, enabling Jansch (and later Renbourn) to establish enviable reputations as solo performers. They first recorded together in 1966, the resulting *Bert And John* LP highlighting the diverse facets of their guitar artistry. Its success paved the way for the formation of a complete group, which duly materialised as Pentangle late in 1967 after its five members had rehearsed at length in Jansch and Renbourn's own folk club, the Three Horseshoes in London's Tottenham Court Road.

Of the other three group members, Jacqui McShee (vocals) had previously worked the folk clubs in a double act with her sister and had also contributed vocals to Renbourn's *Another Monday* (1967). Danny Thompson (bass) and Terry Cox (drums), meanwhile, were accomplished session musicians who had previously played together with Alexis Korner's Blues Incorporated.

Uncharted waters

One of the many nebulous musical terms in vogue in 1967 was 'fusion'. Pentangle's *raison d'être* was to combine elements of blues, jazz and gospel under the umbrella of folk; in a word, fusion music. The group was thus an ambitious attempt to take contemporary music into uncharted waters. The concept was an interesting one; Jansch and Renbourn could sink their own prestigious names into the group, while Jo Lustig was adept at hustling publicity. Their debut album, *The Pentangle* (1968), released to coincide with the group's launch, served merely as an introduction. As they toured the United Kingdom, so the sheer quality of their live performances excited audience expectations for their next recorded work.

Sweet Child (1968) was a double album – a relatively rare occurrence in those days, testifying to the group's growing popularity. Double albums were, even then, frequently excuses for self-indulgence, but in Pentangle's case this extra room for manoeuvre was essential, since it enabled them to present a range of material that adequately reflected the singularly broad repertoire of their stage act.

Above: Pentangle bring their folk sounds to pop television. The group was formed in 1967 around the talents of guitarists John Renbourn (inset above) and Bert Jansch (inset far right) who were both prime exponents of the 'folk baroque' tradition. Jacqui McShee (inset above right), a veteran of the folk club circuit, provided the group with a sweet, unaffected voice.

got to a hit single, but its main impact was in stimulating sales of the album, which reached Number 5 in the charts just before Christmas 1969. Since the opposition included the Beatles' *Abbey Road* and the Rolling Stones' *Let It Bleed*, this was a considerable achievement.

The album – produced, like its predecessor, by Shel Talmy – was delightful in every respect, and fully merited its commercial success. As it transpired, however, it represented the apex of the group's fortunes. After that, they found it impossible either to develop their material or to increase their audience still further. They continued to be a headline attraction throughout 1970, though audiences were beginning to feel a sense of *déjà vu*, and that year's release, *Cruel Sister*, was a disappointment. In truth, the fusion idea had simply reached a logical conclusion. The group had never really achieved a fresh musical synthesis – they had just performed songs from different traditions consecutively, a fact that the introduction of electric guitar failed to conceal.

Solomon's judgement

Like many other folk-based acts, Pentangle fell victim to a creative dissatisfaction that sapped the confidence and resolution of the group members. Undoubtedly, it also had something to do with the inbuilt resistance of the UK audience to folk-oriented acts. Certainly, Jo Lustig – who went on to manage Steeleye Span, Fairport Convention (briefly) and the Chieftains, among others – would later experience exactly the same frustrations of being able to take these groups so far but no further.

In 1972 Pentangle switched labels to Reprise, a move that came too late to rekindle their popularity. Although that year's *Solomon's Seal* magnificently reasserted the group's traditional strengths, the critics treated it harshly and the public neglected it. The group fulfilled their remaining engagements before going their separate ways in March 1973. Danny Thompson went on to record and tour with John Martyn on several occasions, despite increasing health problems. Renbourn and McShee made a faltering attempt to put together a new group in 1974 – one that would have included Indian musicians – but the scheme was abandoned after a disappointing debut at the Cambridge Folk Festival.

Pentangle reformed in 1982, with all the original members, again for the Cambridge Folk Festival. Their period of influence had long since passed, however, and the reformation attracted a bare minimum of interest.

BOB WOFFINDEN

Majority rules

The strengths of the band – the individual instrumental artistry and a strong affinity with a variety of musical traditions – were clearly focused. However diverse the influences, it was a cohesive work in which nothing seemed out of place, and it undoubtedly established the band in the top echelon of British groups. Indeed, they were the first alumni of the folk clubs to break through nationally and exchange a large minority audience for a significant majority one.

Basket Of Light was released in 1969 and contained 'Light Flight', the theme music of 'Take Three Girls', BBC-TV's first colour drama series. The song received considerable airplay and was the nearest the group

Pentangle
Recommended Listening

Sweet Child (Transatlantic TRA 178) (Includes: Goodbye Pork Pie Hat, No More My Lord, The Time Has Come, Sweet Child, The Trees They Do Grow High, Moondog, Sovay).

HATS OFF TO HARPER

Roy Harper: minstrel, misfit and genius

ROY HARPER is arguably British rock's longest-running underground attraction. Since he first strummed his way to public attention via the mid-Sixties folk scene his career has been a perplexing mixture of missed opportunity and sheer perversity. Every time he has seemed on the verge of a commercial breakthrough he has either been stricken by ill-health or opted for temporary retirement in the face of alleged public hostility. Like many of rock's self-styled outlaws, Harper has not been slow to adopt the role of martyr.

Yet his music has much to commend it. In common with that of Kevin Ayers or Robert Wyatt, it has an eccentricity that is thoroughly British; it is no coincidence that, like them, he has been unable to milk the lucrative American rock market (though he has made repeated efforts to do so). He remains very much a musician's musician. The often rambling melodic structure of his songs, the originality and complexity of his lyrics and his fiercely left-wing political stance have attracted a relatively small, though devoted, following. His commitment to his work is undeniable. As he said in an interview with *Rolling Stone* in June 1969: 'When I go to the States this summer I'm going to sit in front of an audience and sing "I Hate The White Man", knowing that probably someone in the audience will get up and aim a gun at my head. But unless you can put your blood on the streets, you're not worth what you're saying.'

Folk outlaw

While many who came up through the folk clubs of the mid Sixties abandoned their creative integrity or just lost their inspiration in the changing climate of the early Seventies, Harper expanded his music and showed that he was as convincing on stage with an electric band as he was playing solo with just guitar accompaniment. But then Harper was always something of an anomaly on the folk scene. His attitude towards his music had more in common with rock than with folk musicians; the folk circuit merely gave him somewhere to play where he'd be tolerated – or not, as the case may be. As he has said: 'I was never really in with that mob. I spent most of my time being thrown out of folk clubs for not being Ralph McTell.'

He had a difficult childhood: 'I think most of my problems can be traced back to the very heavy home scene I had when I was a child,' he later recalled, 'We had fights all the time.' He was born in Manchester on 12 June 1941. His mother died in childbirth and he was brought up by his stepmother, a Jehovah's Witness. Harper has been hostile to religion ever since; as he sings on 'The Spirit Lives', a track from 1975's *HQ*: 'The history of religion is the history of the state/Incestuous exploitation of a catalogue of hate.'

At 15 he was so keen to leave home that he joined the RAF. Within months he decided service life was not for him; to get out he feigned madness. He was discharged but wound up in a psychiatric hospital, where he was given electric shock treatment. 'Committed', a song from his first album, *The Sophisticated Beggar* (1966), alludes to this period. He subsequently attended a group therapy centre, was a patient at Lancaster Moor Mental Institute, and then had trouble with the law, being sent to prison on at least two occasions.

Like so many Fifties kids, Harper had started playing skiffle as an adolescent. He had played at camp concerts while in the RAF, and on his release from jail he started busking. In the summer of 1964 he did the obligatory 'On the Road' trek around Europe and had written enough good material by the time he returned to get a residency at Les Cousins, the Soho folk club where singers like Bert Jansch, John Renbourn and Al Stewart all served their apprenticeships.

It was with the release of Harper's second album, *Come Out Fighting Genghis Smith* (1967), that he began to win attention. Though not a commercial success, it provided in embryonic form the qualities that would gain him his reputation as the country's 'paramount stoned freak poet'. 'Freak Street', an impression of Soho, 'Ageing Raver' and 'You Don't Need Money' highlighted Harper's surreal humour; 'Circle', running for a then almost unprecedented 11 minutes, and the eight-minute title cut were ambitious, declamatory, loosely structured songs. As he told an interviewer at the time: 'Some of my songs start out nice and suburbia and suddenly swing violently across to anarchy.' Despite its shortcomings the album – subsequently re-released on CBS' Embassy budget label as *The Early Years* – had much to commend it.

Its successor, *Folkjokeopus* (1969), confirmed Harper as an original if erratic songwriter-guitarist. Unfortunately this originality tended to work against him as far as commercial success was concerned, his music having few obvious antecedents. He was a regular performer at the series of free concerts that took place in London's Hyde Park in the late Sixties, but even in the burgeoning 'progressive' climate of the time he failed to win the admiration of more than a dedicated few. To them Harper's onstage unpredictability, which included engaging in furious arguments with the audience, proved that here was a

Top right: Roy Harper on stage with famous friend Jimmy Page, 1974. Right: Harper goes electric with his band Trigger at the Knebworth Festival, 1975.

performer who wasn't just out for what he could get. For Harper, professionalism appeared to be the kiss of death.

Indictments of the state

Harper's fourth record label change came in 1970 when he released his first album for Harvest, EMI's newly-formed label for 'underground' acts (Harvest also had Pink Floyd on its books). Harper's association with the label was to last ten years. *Flat, Baroque And Berserk* (1970) featured two songs that were to become classics in Harper's repertoire – 'I Hate The White Man' and 'McGoohan's Blues'. The latter took its inspiration from the television series, 'The Prisoner', starring Patrick McGoohan as the victim of a futuristic state where the forces of repression reign supreme. 'I Hate The White Man' was a blistering attack on Western materialism, racism and authoritarianism with a sideswipe at God thrown in: 'I hate the white man/And his plastic excuse/I hate the man/And his plastic excuse/I hate the white man/And the man who turned him loose.'

Harper, as has already been noted, had never been short of originality. On his next album, *Stormcock* (1971), his musical vision came into its own. Containing just four cuts, *Stormcock* showed him at the height of his powers as a writer and performer. Aided by producer Peter Jenner, he explored the possibilities of the recording studio for the first time in his career. With guitars, keyboards, vocals and on one track, 'Me And My Woman', the superlative string arrangements of David Bedford, Harper succeeded in creating a multi-textured patchwork of sound.

Listening to the album, it is not difficult to understand why Led Zeppelin's Jimmy Page, who plays guitar on this and many of his subsequent recordings, speaks so highly of Harper. The music had the same expansive quality that Zeppelin have achieved on occasion, regardless of the enormous differences in style between the two acts. 'Me And My Woman', in particular, was generous, adventurous rock music at its best. The mix of Bedford's strings and Harper's vigorous guitar work might have seemed inappropriate, but the end effect was sublime, the song having a deceptive mellifluence and lyricism that is all too rare in rock.

Stormcock did not sell as well as it deserved to do, and whatever commercial chances Harper had at this stage of his career were ruined by ill-health; his acting debut in a film, *Made* (1972), did not do much to raise his public stock either. His illness, a circulation disorder, was serious enough to warrant speculation about his imminent demise. However, he released his next album, *Lifemask*, in 1973 and that same year returned to live work. More elaborately arranged than its predecessor, *Lifemask* was exceptional for the apocalyptic 'The Lord's Prayer', which covered an entire side.

The subsequent *Valentine* (1971) was, by comparison, more conventional. Appropriately *Valentine* was an album of love songs, yet as 'Forbidden Fruit' showed, Harper had not veered towards the middle of the road. To promote the record he took the unexpected step of exploiting the esteem in which he was held by fellow rock musicians by playing a gig at London's Rainbow Theatre with an all-star backing band including Jimmy Page, Keith Moon and Ronnie Lane.

To be fair, Harper must have been feeling frustrated with the musical limitations of playing as a solo act, for he was soon to form his first band, Trigger. The band featured such high-calibre musicians as drummer Bill Bruford, formerly of Yes and King Crimson, and guitarist Chris Spedding, a veteran of numerous sessions and of the ill-starred Sharks.

Trigger happy

Harper and Trigger struck up an uncanny chemistry, playing a particularly striking set at the Knebworth Festival in 1975 when they supported Pink Floyd. If anyone had ever doubted Harper's ability to play and write rock'n'roll, Trigger should have convinced them otherwise. The album Harper made with Trigger, *HQ* (1975), echoed the greatness of *Stormcock*, albeit in a different way. The opening 'The Game' featured Harper's by now familiar stream-of-consciousness lyrics, but this time the collage of sound, underpinned by an archetypal rock riff, showcased some quite exceptional musicianship, notably from Messrs Bruford and Spedding. Elsewhere 'Grown Ups Are Just Silly Children' served as a reminder that Harper's didacticism has always been offset by a sense of fun. The album concluded with 'When An Old Cricketer Leaves The Crease', a beautiful piece of English nostalgia featuring David Bedford's haunting brass arrangement.

Potentially Harper was now in a position to establish himself as the major talent he so patently was. Instead, defiant to the

last, he announced his decision to quit Britain for America, blaming public apathy in his own land. Two years later Harper released *Bullinamingvase* (1977), which in 'One Of Those Days In England' contained Harper's most commercial song yet. Not only did it have a catchy hook, it also featured the McCartneys chirping away on backing vocals. 'One Of Those Days In England' was a minor hit and the album was critically acclaimed, but fate was not on Harper's side – he was hospitalised following speculation that he had caught a rare disease after reputedly giving the kiss of life to one of his sheep on his Herefordshire farm.

Harper recovered (the complaint was, in fact, a recurrence of his earlier problem) but appeared to lose his creative momentum; EMI rejected his next album, *Commercial Break*, and it was not until 1980 that he resurfaced with *The Unknown Soldier*. Harper continued to produce idiosyncratic albums throughout the Eighties. 1985's *Whatever Happened To Jugula?* paired him with Jimmy Page and made the bottom of the LP charts—but few were prompted to ask 'Whatever Happened To Roy Harper?' STEVE CLARKE

Left: One of those days in England – a self-styled 'outlaw of rock' poses by a window.
Below: One of those days in France – Harper plays Paris, 1977.

Roy Harper
Recommended Listening

Harper 1970-1975 (Harvest SHSM 2025) (Includes: I Hate The White Man, Tom Tiddler's Ground, When An Old Cricketer Leaves The Crease, Don't You Grieve, Another Day, South Africa).

Sounds of Subversion

**Discord and confrontation epitomised
the flipside of the US rock scene**

As the Sixties drew to a close, the prevailing trend of the musical mainstream was towards conservatism, compromise and complacency, with 'progressive' celebrations of technical virtuosity on the one hand and the soft self-analysis of the singer-songwriters on the other. Its reflection of the increasingly introspective mood of youth saw rock grow less challenging and more comfortable as the excitement, versatility and spirit of 1966 and 1967 descended into stagnation. Yet while the majority was content to soothe and flatter, there were still those whose music, whether by satire, cynicism, outrage or overt nihilism, represented confrontation.

The music and performance of artists like Frank Zappa and the Mothers of Invention, Captain Beefheart and his Magic Band, the MC5 and Iggy and the Stooges – along with the bleak visions of the Velvet Underground and the disturbing avant-garde work of such acts as

Iggy Pop goose-steps into the spotlight. In 1969, the music of Iggy and the Stooges was described as 'a reductio ad absurdum of rock'n'roll' – a description with which the nihilistic singer never quibbled.

the Godz and Autosalvage – would ensure that the ideals of social and cultural conflict essential to the spirit of rock'n'roll would survive the post-Woodstock malaise.

Revolt and rebellion

At a time when the average rock show was a static affair – electric guitarists standing in the spotlight, contorting their faces to fit their 'licks', or self-conscious solo artistes perched on stools, baring their souls – the live acts of these unorthodox American subversives offered *theatre*: from the flag-ripping of the MC5 to the flesh-slashing of Iggy Pop, from the bizarre costumes and twitching limbs of the Magic Band to US Marines bayonetting dolls with Frank Zappa. Although there was no common link between the sound of these various acts, they were united, nonetheless, by perversity and by their refusal to conform to the constraints of the new rock industry.

Above: Frank Zappa strikes a characteristically absurd pose. Through his parodies of the American way of life and his unmerciful lampoons of youth culture, Zappa showed himself to be the ultimate cynic of rock.

'The behaviour of rock stars, the mode of the music and the attitudes of many of its fans are unequivocally subversive,' wrote Richard Neville in *Playpower*, his 1970 book on underground culture, 'but the product is packaged and marketed by the establishment, at dizzy profits for all involved, and has failed to transform the world into a Battleship Potemkin.' Although the hippie idealism of San Francisco had been absorbed, diluted and re-promoted in less potent forms by the industry, the ever-increasing violence of cities such as New York and Detroit sparked off a rock sound that had more in common with personal revolt than cosmic rebellion.

In 1967, the streets of Detroit flared up in riots; the following year saw the MC5 record their first album, *Kick Out The Jams* – an LP of raw, uncompromising, modern rock'n'roll that captured the essence of the brutal urban sound. The politics of the MC5, based on the revolutionary philosophies of their manager John Sinclair, were naive to say the least. ('We are FREE; we are a bunch of arrogant mother-lovers and we don't give a damn for any cop or any kind of phony authority control-addict creep who wants to put us down. We demand total freedom for everybody!' Sinclair was given to ranting.) But the aggression and energy of their untutored heavy metal gave no quarter; harsh and unrelenting, the MC5 were undoubtedly at odds with the mellowing mood of the times.

Those other uncontrollable sons of the Motor City, Iggy and the Stooges, lacked any sense of revolutionary values or political ideals – their sound, and Iggy's stage act, was founded on wild depravity, animal sexuality, unfettered nihilism and abuse of self and the audience. When Iggy slapped his own face with his silver lamé gloves he was slapping the crowd, demanding a reaction.

Reviewing the group's first album, *The Stooges*, in 1969, *Rolling Stone* critic Ed Ward described the music as 'a *reductio ad absurdum* of rock'n'roll that might have been thought up by a mad general in a wet dream.' Or as journalist Lester Bangs put it years later: 'The Stooges' music was brutal, mindless, primitive, vicious, base, savage, primal, hate-filled, grungy, terrifying and above all REAL.'

Frank speaking

While Detroit audiences were confronted by Iggy's three dumb chords, noise, sleaze, arrogance and self-mutilation, Los Angeles' Mothers of Invention elicited reactions with weird and garish montages of avant-garde complexity, savage humour, filth and rock'n'roll parody. At the root of Frank Zappa's work was a love/hate relationship with all aspects of contemporary culture – sex, hypocrisy, money, war, power, ethnic minorities, religion and food – and an ill-disguised contempt for American youth.

Zappa was, in many ways, rock's ultimate

cynic and nihilist. 'The whole hippie scene is wishful thinking,' he said in 1968. 'They wish they could love but they're full of it. It's easier to make someone mad than to make somebody love.' So whereas, according to Zappa, the rest of the music scene was 'promoting a love relationship between the audience and the group – the group is supposed to love the audience to death', the Mothers of Invention went out of their way to exhibit disdain, deride their audience, confuse them and often alienate them altogether. 'Hello pigs!' Zappa would snarl in greeting as he took the stage.

The group's music was never relaxing and could be downright anarchic. 'Half the time when we're really doing something, the audience doesn't know what it is,' commented Zappa in 1968. 'Last week we were playing in Philadelphia and we got seven requests so we played them all at the same time. The audience couldn't even tell the songs apart.'

Out come the freaks

The music of Zappa protégé Captain Beefheart, meanwhile, was equally bizarre and inaccessible. But whereas Zappa plundered jazz, teen doo-wop and avant-garde classical forms to create his jaded anti-American commercials, Beefheart was more original and less cynical. The complexity of his music and the scintillating instrumental interplay of his Magic Band combined with his surrealistic wit to provide bizarre visions of life that were passionate and inspired. And yet, given the bland temper of the times, there were few who took Beefheart seriously. Fewer still could come to terms with the demands of his music; even Frank Zappa – much to the Captain's disgust – took to promoting him as a gruffer version of Tiny Tim.

In the end, these late-Sixties US subversives were operating in a vacuum; none were to be rewarded with much commercial success and none were able to affect rock's trend towards respectability. Looking back on the era in 1977, albeit with the benefit of hindsight and a surfeit of scathing contumely, Lester Bangs summed up their contributions thus: 'It was obvious that the fun was beginning to go out of the rock scene as early as 1968 and by 1971 it had fallen completely apart, leaving us with James Taylor, the all-time simpy narcissistic snotrich phony-angst introspective idiot.'

But despite the sterilisation of rock, the spirit of Iggy Pop, the MC5, Zappa *et al* would not be forgotten. It was their sound and attitudes that would pave the way for the mid-Seventies outrage and shock tactics of such acts as Alice Cooper and the New York Dolls. And when the Sex Pistols sparked off the British punk movement in 1976, it was the US subversives of the late Sixties that would provide much of the inspiration.   TOM HIBBERT

Above: The MC5 – radical hippies before their national flag. On stage, the group would tear the Stars and Stripes to pieces in anti-establishment defiance. Below: Captain Beefheart and his Magic Band enjoy their own version of a beach party.

Captain Beefheart: desert songs and magic music

IF SUCCESS in the music business were measured in creativity rather than the ability to please the greatest number of people the most amount of time, then Captain Beefheart would be a rich man indeed. Beefheart's tortuous career in 'showbiz' says as much about the business as it does about the man himself: from his first recordings with the Magic Band in 1965, it was clear that the Captain would not stay happily tethered in any pre-defined corner of the market-place.

Captain Beefheart was born Don Van Vliet in Glendale, California, on 15 January 1941. In this sparsely inhabited locale, referred to on his first album as 'The Desert', Don shared his early years with the blue jay, the jack-rabbit, the coyote and high-school friend Frank Zappa. It was while relaxing in an abandoned car, somewhere in the desert, that Don and Frank decided to make a film together, called *Captain Beefheart Meets The Grunt People*. The film never materialised, but the young Van Vliet adopted the hero's name and became Captain Beefheart.

Milk and Kandy
Early in 1964, after a brief spell singing with a local combo named the Blackouts with Zappa, Beefheart formed the first incarnation of his own Magic Band featuring Alex St Claire and Ry Cooder on guitars, Jerry Handley on bass and Drumbo (real name John French) on drums. Later that year, the group signed to A&M Records and released two flop singles, 'Diddy Wah Diddy' – a cover of the Bo Diddley song – and 'Who Do You Think You're Fooling'. They also recorded an album, but when A&M heard the finished results, they refused to release it – Beefheart's lyrics were, the company thought, just too unconventional for the commercial market. Undaunted, Beefheart took the work to the less staid offices of Kama Sutra, and in 1966 *Safe As Milk* was granted a release on the Buddah label.

Although all the songs on *Safe As Milk* were Beefheart originals, they owed more to Howlin' Wolf and Chicago blues than anything else. Yet despite being steeped in the blues, like so many other songs of the era, there was nothing else orthodox about the music – the Magic Band's sound was unique. The two guitarists played complementary parts – there was no 'lead' or 'rhythm' as such – weaving a jabbing yet crystalline backcloth over which the Captain sang his bizarre, surrealistic lyrics with his splintering bass growl.

Above: The gospel according to Don Van Vliet. Opposite: Hats off to Beefheart.

Produced by Bob Krasnow and Richard Perry, *Safe As Milk* was largely ignored in the US. For while Jefferson Airplane, the Grateful Dead *et al* were lionised by American consumer hippies, Captain Beefheart and his Magic Band, it seemed, were just too undiluted for the mass-market imagination even in those open-minded times. In the UK, however, it was a different story. The LP became an instant 'underground' classic, and Beefheart further enhanced his cult status with devastatingly loud and energetic gigs at London's Middle Earth and Speakeasy clubs in early 1968.

By then, Beefheart's songs were getting longer; the music was just as powerful as before but it was less blues-oriented, more meandering and complex, while the lyrics were funnier and more impressionistic. Ry Cooder had been replaced by Jeff Cotton, who played straggly, wandering guitar, wore a dress and a bowler hat and frequently sat in the bushes making bird noises. Somewhat unsurprisingly, Beefheart and his Magic Band had been filed under 'weird' by the music industry and when a second album, *Strictly Personal*, emerged in the spring of 1968, the Captain discovered, to his disgust, that producer Bob Krasnow had treated the material with extensive phasing to make the music more obviously 'far out'.

Beefheart virtually disowned the album: 'It was butchered while we were in England,' he commented at the time. 'The music was done honestly and shines through like a diamond in the mud.' The album's closing track, 'Kandy Korn', at least, remains a masterpiece. The guitars, chiming yet distorted, hang delicately over a winding abyss of bass and drums that never repeats itself throughout the piece. The band chant 'Be reborn' toward the final, exultant coda and the mood at the end is one of exorcism. 'I ain't blue no more!' testifies Beefheart when it's all over.

Blimp in the spotlight
In mid 1968, the Captain signed with Frank Zappa's Straight label and departed to the desert to prepare a new album. The results were released the following year as *Trout Mask Replica*, a double album of 28 songs all around the three minute mark and all unlike anything anyone had ever heard before. Throughout the LP Beefheart delivered his strange, compelling lyrics over backing tracks where just enough notes were fitted together to convince the listener that the band weren't making it up as they went along.

The dense, abrasive and undiluted songs included a vivid portrayal of atrocity on 'Dachau Blues' – 'Dancing and screaming and dying in the ovens/Coughing smoke and dying by the dozens/Down in Dachau Blues' – and other lurid, disjointed rants against the ferocity of humans, including 'My Human Gets Me Blues', 'Ant Man Bee' and 'Steal Softly Thru Snow'. Meanwhile, a happier side of the Captain surfaced on numbers such as 'The Blimp', a ludicrous falsetto monologue about an old airship covered in nipples, breathlessly intoned over a typewriter bass and yawning sax.

The primal, unearthly quality of *Trout Mask Replica* had been enhanced by the addition, on bass and guitar respectively, of Rockette Morton (real name Mark Boston) and Zoot Horn Rollo (Bill Harkelroad). Jeff Cotton had metamorphosed into Antennae Jimmy Semens and Beefheart's cousin, the Mascara Snake, had been enrolled on bass clarinet. None of the newcomers were experienced musicians, and the band had spent a year in the desert learning to play the *Trout Mask* songs – and, reportedly, indulging in all kinds of psychedelic substances.

By 1970, however, the band's line-up had changed again. Ed Marimba, who as Artie Tripp had been with Zappa's Mothers of Invention, had joined to add percussion while Antennae Jimmy had quit following a fight during which he had broken Rockette's dentures. As a result, the new album, *Lick My Decals Off Baby*, was recorded with only one guitarist; and yet, with its flurrying saxes and tropical marimba runs, the LP proved to be even more of a musical jungle than *Trout Mask Replica*. But, coming so soon after the staggering innovation of its predecessor, the record broke no new ground.

Soon after the 1970 release of *Lick My Decals Off Baby*, producer Frank Zappa and the Captain fell out with one another. After criticising Zappa for promoting him as a freakshow – though, in all fairness, how else could the silent majority have been introduced to his extraordinary sound? – Beefheart signed to Warner/Reprise, recruited a second guitarist in Winged Eel Fingerling (Elliott Ingber) and began work on a fifth album. *The Spotlight Kid* was released in late 1971 and, whether under pressure to reach a bigger audience or simply to cut corners and have a good time, Beefheart came up with his most accessible record since *Safe As Milk*.

The songs were basically one riff played throughout, but created by the inter-relation of all the instruments rather than – as in most 'heavy' bands – by unison guitars and bass. Similarly the rhythms, though repetitive, were far from the Grand Funk/Led Zeppelin thrash that was popular at the time: the Magic Band played a mixture of blues, funk and voodoo that was unique, but just as danceable, and louder than the rest of them.

Live, the group were staggeringly powerful. Rockette Morton would come writhing onto the stage, with an electric toaster on his head, and strum his bass viciously until Zoot Horn Rollo, thin and wispy in a Chinaman's hat, plugged in on the other side and produced a sound that fitted with Rockette's seemingly random attack. When all the other musicians were on stage, the Captain – resplendent in a black and gold cape – would stride imperiously to the microphone and boom 'I'm gonna booglarize you, baby!' into the already groaning PA. The whole band jived relentlessly throughout the set, Beefheart chased Rockette Morton around like an escaped turkey and the assembled musicians reproduced their leader's compositions – new and old – note for note. What had sounded too cranky for many people on record made perfect sense live.

In 1972, the ranks of the Magic Band shifted yet again; Fingerling quit, Morton transferred to guitar and Orejon (Roy Estrada, another ex-Mother) took over on bass. On *Clear Spot*, produced by Ted Templeman and released later that year, the rhythm section veered towards syncopated, loping funk, the guitars became more elaborate and the occasional use of horns and female backing vocals added an element of soul music. Many of the songs were celebrations of sexual love and, from the rousing 'Nowadays A Woman's Gotta Hit A Man' to the exquisite 'Her Eyes Are A Blue Million Miles', Beefheart made love songs seem more alive than they had in years. If there was any point in his career when Beefheart could have crossed over into the million-selling bracket, this was it. A world tour in 1973 was a sellout and Captain Beefheart and his Magic Band seemed only inches away from mass acceptance. But in 1974 disaster struck.

The list of Beefheart's record companies and musicians is a long one; likewise his

advisers and managers. Though a domineering character on stage, he was easily influenced when it came to business matters. Thus it was that Andy Di Martino, who had recently become involved with the Beefheart entourage, persuaded him to record *Unconditionally Guaranteed*, an album of short poppy songs written by the Captain, his wife Janet and Di Martino himself. The cover shot of Beefheart clutching two fistfuls of dollars summed up the intention of the record, but the reality was too half-hearted and laid-back to make it a commercial success. Although some of the tracks, like 'Peaches' and 'Upon The My-O-My' were likeable enough, the Magic Band was wasted on such lightweight material. On the eve of Beefheart's third British tour in 1974, his Magic Band all quit, leaving him to stumble through the dates backed by a very average band called Buckwheat that was dredged up at the last moment.

Divided we fall . . .

Although Beefheart claimed that he composed and arranged all his music, the departing Magic Band complained at Beefheart taking all the credit when they themselves had contributed a fair amount. And it was undeniable that without a *bona fide* Magic Band, the Captain's stage show was half what it had been. On the other hand, when Harkelroad, Boston and Tripp (now shorn of their exotic stage names) formed a band called Mallard in 1975, they couldn't come up with anything very original either.

Meanwhile the Captain was still under the influence of Di Martino, and mortgaged what remained of his credibility to make *Bluejeans And Moonbeams*, a collection of pleasant and thoroughly disposable numbers, with a bunch of session men in late 1974. Beefheart now seemed to be leaning over backwards to become someone else – a faceless artist for a faceless public. The creative spark appeared to have died. 1975 saw a drunken Beefheart humiliating himself by singing Frank Zappa's lyrics in Zappa's band, although he was allowed to recite one or two of his own poems during the intervals. But 1976 saw a miraculous return to form with a new LP, *Bat Chain Puller*.

After a year's inactivity, Beefheart had amassed a collection of new songs that reflected the many styles he had pioneered over the previous 10 years. From the title track – the metronomic tale of some enormous phallic slug oozing through the desert, decked with coloured lights – to the ominous parable of social collapse, 'The Thousand And Tenth Day Of The Human Totem Pole' with its *Trout Mask*-like guitars and stumbling rhythm section, the music was a conscious return to classic Magic Band style.

Because of typically convoluted managerial problems, however – Beefheart's contract was disputed between Virgin, Warners and Mercury – *Bat Chain Puller* could not be released. And by the

time he was legally in a position to release a record, Beefheart had updated the album, re-recording five of the original tracks and adding six new ones. The result, *Shiny Beast*, was released in late 1978 – on Warners in the US and on Virgin in the UK – and although some of the new tracks were excellent, notably the African-style 'Tropical Hot Dog Night', the music lacked the appeal of the original 1976 tape.

By now a new Magic Band, comprised of newcomers Robert Williams on drums, Jeff Morris Tepper on guitar and Eric Drew Feldman on bass, had stabilised and a new album, *Doc At The Radar Station*, emerged in 1980. Although the music was Beefheart's most complex since *Lick My Decals Off Baby* and the lyrics were as vivid as ever, the overall sound was somewhat dry and arid – inspired, but no longer happy. On tour during the winter of 1980-81, Beefheart seemed like an angry old man – still magnetic but no longer as expansive

as the cloaked supremo of yore. And it was strange to watch him on stage with musicians who looked young enough to be his children playing the licks popularised a decade earlier.

The 1982 album, *Ice Cream For Crow*, showed that Captain Beefheart still had much to offer, however. Although his music was no longer innovative, it still contained an irrepressible wit, bite and imagination.

Although Beefheart had deserted music for art by the late Eighties (and was claiming to make more money from it), echoes of his pioneering work were still audible. The Captain was clearly ahead of his time.

LUTHER PAISLEY

Whether in tearful mood (right), giving his detractors the bird (far right) or in his element on stage (below), Captain Beefheart could always be relied upon to entertain.

**Captain Beefheart
Recommended Listening**

Safe As Milk (Pye International NPL 28110) (Includes: Dropout Boogie, Electricity, Yellow Brick Road, Abba Zaba, Plastic Factory, Autumn's Child); *Clear Spot* (Reprise K54007) (Includes: Low Yo Yo Stuff, Nowadays A Woman's Gotta Hit A Man, My Head Is My Only House Unless It Rains, Her Eyes Are A Blue Million Miles, Big Eyed Beans From Venus, Golden Birdies).

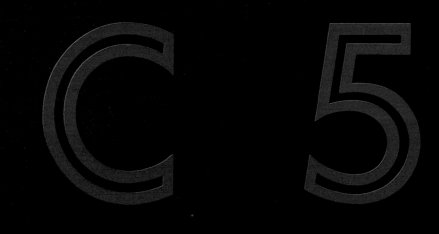

Kicking out the jams with the Motor City rebels

'IF YOU TAKE EVERYTHING in the universe and break it down to a common denominator, all you've got is energy,' said the MC5's Wayne Kramer in 1969. 'It's the level we communicate from – that's the essence of the urban sound.' In the late Sixties, when much American music was mellowing, the MC5 peddled uncompromising, high-energy rock. Blended with radical hippie politics and naive idealism, it echoed the street tension of their native Detroit. But although the group's frantic stage shows – hectic heavy metal and rabble-rousing anarchy – won support from proto-punks and the counter-culture, they were just too unrelenting to be accepted by the Woodstock generation as a whole.

The Motor City Five, as they were originally known, were formed in Detroit in 1966 by Rob Tyner (vocals), Michael Davis (bass), Dennis Thompson (drums) and guitarists Wayne Kramer and Fred 'Sonic' Smith. Initially an R&B/soul outfit playing around the clubs of Detroit and Ann Arbor, the group soon acquired a reputation for showing up at gigs drunk, late or not at all, playing too loud and being sick on Beatles albums. By the summer of 1967, the band had released one unsuccessful single, 'One Of The Guys', on the local AMG label and had been banned from all but the sleaziest local venues. Then, after a rare appearance at Northville's Cavern (where the Motor City Five lost to the Unrelated Segments in a 'Battle Of The Bands' contest), the group were approached by John Sinclair, who offered to manage them.

Despite his lack of managerial experience, Sinclair set to work acquiring new equipment and soon the MC5 were playing regularly at Detroit's Grande Ballroom for 125 dollars a night. But Sinclair wasn't merely a rock fan – he was also 'Minister of Information' for the radical hippie White Panther party. Under Sinclair's guidance, the MC5 began to move away from R&B/soul towards high-volume rock'n'roll with a strong anti-establishment accent.

In October 1967, the MC5 released a second single, 'Looking At You', on the local A-Square label. The record captured the group's raw, frenetic style perfectly

Below: The MC5's guitarists Fred 'Sonic' Smith (left) and Wayne Kramer address an audience with the White Panthers' salute. Inset: Peace-sign propaganda on a 1969 gig poster.

'The MC5 is totally committed to the revolution. With our music and our economic genius we plunder the unsuspecting straight world for money and the means to carry out our program and revolutionise its children at the same time . . . We are bad . . . We will use guns if we have to—we will do anything if we have to.'

John Sinclair, 1969

and began to pick up airplay on Detroit's 'underground' radio station WABX.

On 7 June 1968, the MC5 supported Cream at the Grande Ballroom. They turned in a devastating set that, claimed Sinclair, 'destroyed Cream so totally that Cream didn't even know it'. As the MC5 reached the feedback-growling climax of 'Black To Comm', Tyner ripped an American flag to pieces, provoking an orgy of cheers. 'People were rolling around, moaning in ecstasy on the floor,' Sinclair recalled. 'It was the most intense moment in the history of rock and roll.'

Kick Out The Jams, recorded at the Grande in October 1968 and released the following year on Elektra, showed that Sinclair's enthusiasm for MC5 live was not completely misplaced. From the berserk treatment of the standard 'Ramblin' Rose' to Fred Smith's stampeding interpretation of Detroit's 1967 riots, 'Motor City Is Burning', the power of the rhythm section combined with the twin-guitar attack and Tyner's exultant, clawing vocals to create a sound of unparalleled force.

By the time the album was released, the MC5 were already notorious. In March 1969, the underground paper *Berkeley Barb* had been prosecuted for publishing a photograph of group members committing indecent acts with a female member of the White Panthers. The album caused further outrage with its unprintable opening shout. Its obscene message meant a record store refused to stock the album and the group retaliated by covering the shop front with obscene stickers. Elektra's response was to drop the MC5 and alter the offending lines to 'Kick out the jams, brothers and sisters' on all subsequent copies of the LP they released.

Back in the USA

Late in 1969, Sinclair was arrested for possession of two marijuana cigarettes and put on trial in Ann Arbor. Despite Michigan's liberal drug laws, Judge Colombo sentenced Sinclair – 'a person,' he proclaimed, 'who has deliberately flaunted and scoffed at the law' – to 10 years' imprisonment. Sinclair's 'revolution' would be suppressed behind bars. The stance of the White Panthers, which had seemed credible in 1967 and 1968, seemed unrealistic and self-defeating by 1969. The MC5, now signed to Atlantic, began to replace their old political anthems with songs that dealt with the problems of a new teenage generation.

Back In The USA (1970), produced by rock critic Jon Landau, was crammed with three-minute gems such as 'High School', 'American Ruse' and 'Teenage Lust' on which the uncontrolled hysteria of old made way for a more refined fervour, with twin guitars and racing rhythm section working overtime. To old MC5 fans, however, the album seemed like a compromise, while it attracted few new devotees. The 1971 album *High Time* saw the band's previous drive and conviction diluted by the addition of mass brass, and in 1972, following a disastrous European tour, the MC5 disbanded. Rob Tyner made various attempts to front a new MC5 line up, Fred 'Sonic' Smith drifted off to the bland hard rock of his own Sonics Rendezvous, Michael Davis languished in prison following a drugs arrest and Wayne Kramer followed him after attempting to sell cocaine to a policewoman in 1976.

The punk boom of the late Seventies, however, was to bring a belated recognition for the style, verve and energy of the MC5; while the recordings of the long-defunct group were re-released, the hectic frenzy of their early stage shows was emulated by countless acts. In a letter from prison in the early Seventies, John Sinclair had described the atmosphere of an early MC5 performance. His words might have been equally applicable to any number of punk groups playing in London in 1976-77: 'It was a beautiful demonstration of the principles of high-energy performance: as the performer puts out more, the energy level of the audience is raised – and they give back more energy to the performers until everything is TOTALLY FRENZIED.'   TOM HIBBERT

> **MC5**
> **Recommended Listening**
>
> *Kick Out The Jams* (Elektra K42027) (Includes: Kick Out The Jams, Ramblin' Rose, Borderline, Motor City Is Burning, I Want You Right Now, Rocket Reducer No. 62 (Rama Lama Fa Fa Fa)); *Back In The USA* (Atlantic K50346) (Includes: High School, Back In The USA, American Ruse, Call Me Animal, Teenage Lust).

ZAPPA

FRANK ZAPPA was born a composer. Had he been born in a different time or place, he would probably have become a 'serious' composer. But fortunately for rock music he grew up in the teen culture of California listening to Fifties doowop and R&B, and these were the styles that would permeate his compositions. From his early work onwards, Zappa evolved for himself an enormously flexible musical language that could encompass everything from atonal orchestral passages to humorous dialogue, and he developed a unique musical format that required highly trained musicians who could sight-read and respond to hand signals. This in turn made the ever-changing Zappa band one of the great rock 'n'roll training grounds (comparable to the big bands before the war), while a theatrical veneer to his shows enabled him to present material that might normally have been too complex for a rock audience.

As one of the first to attempt to merge pop, rock, jazz and classical music, Zappa has, arguably, extended the boundaries of

Surreal anarchy from the Mother superior

rock'n'roll more than any other performer. If anything has prevented his work being accorded its due place, then it must be its sheer magnitude: few, if any, rock artists have been so prolific or sustained such creative energy over such a timespan.

On 21 December 1940, a Sicilian-Greek couple in Baltimore, Maryland, had their first child. They called him Frank (not Francis) Zappa after his father and followed him with Bob, Carl and Candy. When Frank was nine, the family moved to Monterey, California, and three years later to Pomona, a suburb of Los Angeles. Frank senior worked in the missile industry, first for Convair, then for Lockheed, and this meant constantly moving home: from LA to San Diego, then to Lancaster, California, a small town in the Mojave Desert.

Zappa's teenage years were spent listen-

ing to the radio – the sounds of the Penguins, Johnny Otis, the Teen Queens, the Shields, the Rays, the Clovers and all the many other doowop and R&B groups – at a time when status at high school depended on wearing the right sort of shoes and sex was something you did in cars. Constant moving had made Frank a bit of a loner with no close friends so he was pleased to meet and befriend Don Van Vliet, later Captain Beefheart, at the Antelope Valley High School. They used to sit up all night listening to records and have to skip school the next day in order to sleep.

In 1956 Zappa formed a school combo called the Blackouts, an eight-piece in which he played guitar. By then he had

Above left: Portrait of the artist . . . Inset above right: The Mothers of Invention. From left, background: Billy Mundi, Jimmy Carl Black, Roy Estrada, Buck Gardner, Don Preston. Foreground: Zappa and Ray Collins. Right: Bandleader Zappa plays lead guitar.

already discovered modern 'classical' music, particularly Edgard Varèse and Igor Stravinsky; he played Varèse's *Ionization* over and over till Rosemarie, his mother, banned it from the living room. On his fifteenth birthday he spent the money he was given as a present on a telephone call to Varèse in New York City. Between the ages of 14 and 18 he wrote a huge amount of music, most of which he was never to hear performed since it required an orchestra.

The world's greatest sinner

Early in 1959 Frank Zappa senior was on the move again. This time Frank did not accompany his parents. Instead, he took an apartment in the Echo Park section of Los Angeles, a bohemian area near the Hollywood Freeway, and wrote the score for a low-budget Western movie, *Run Home Slow*, which was scripted by his old English teacher. However, the movie folded during production when the lead actress miscarried on the second day of shooting, and Frank moved back to the suburbs.

In Alta Loma, out near the San Gabriel Mountains, Zappa enrolled in Chaffee Junior College where he studied harmony and married his first wife, Kay. He soon dropped out of school, however, and while Kay worked in a bank, Frank played cocktail music in bars for 20 dollars a night and worked as the art director of a greeting card company by day.

In 1960 he wrote the music for another B movie, *The World's Greatest Sinner*; using a 52-piece (mainly amateur) orchestra, he recorded it at Chaffee College, mixing it down to mono in a truck parked outside. It was Frank's first orchestral piece to be performed. He never got paid.

While Frank kept on writing, he and Kay struggled to survive until, in 1963, *Run Home Slow* went back into production. With his share of the advance money Frank bought his first real electric guitar and also acquired a home-made five-track recording studio in nearby Cucamonga. He changed its name to Studio Z and opened for business charging 13 dollars 50 cents an hour. He got few takers but certainly put all that free studio time to good use,

recording hours of experimental music with Don Van Vliet. By 1964, Zappa had split up with Kay and was living in the studio with his friend Jim 'Motorhead' Sherwood and two girls.

Memories of El Monte

San Bernardino County is notoriously conservative, and the goings-on at Studio Z did not go unnoticed. One day a used car salesman asked Frank if he could come up with a sex tape for a little party he was giving for the boys – something X-rated, Frank would know. Frank knew. He also knew that the 100-dollar fee would buy a lot of food and tape, so he and one of the girls bounced up and down on the squeaky bed, recorded a lot of sexy conversation, edited out all the laughing, recorded some accompanying movie music and mixed the whole lot together. The next day the man called for his tape. He showed them his badge. He was Detective Willis of the San Bernardino Vice Squad. Frank had been set up. He spent 10 days in jail, three years on probation and was exempted from the draft for being an ex-con. He bailed the girl out using advance royalties on 'Memories Of El Monte', a song that he and Ray Collins had written for the Penguins.

The many moods of Frank Zappa: at the microphone (left), with guitar (below), and raising an umbrella indoors, defying rumours of impending ill-fortune (opposite).

1492

Messed Up My Mind (1969) and on the GTOs' *Permanent Damage* (1969), which he also produced. He recorded Wild Man Fischer, an eccentric who had hitherto sung songs for dimes on the streets of Hollywood, and edited and issued albums by such great spoken-word artists as Lenny Bruce and Lord 'The Nazz' Buckley.

These releases showed Zappa's continuing interest in LA street culture, both teen and underground. (This interest re-emerged in 1982 when he recorded a duet called 'Valley Girl' with his daughter Moon Unit, which parodied the language of the teenage girls of the San Fernando Valley.) But Zappa's greatest achievement during this period was the production of Captain Beefheart's classic *Trout Mask Replica* album.

Hot peaches

By now Frank had moved to the top of Laurel Canyon, and during August and September 1969 he worked on his second solo album with the help of a host of musicians including Ian Underwood (keyboards and woodwind), Shuggie Otis (bass), John Guerin (drums), violinists Don 'Sugarcane' Harris and Jean-Luc Ponty, and Captain Beefheart, who contributed growling vocals to 'Willie The Pimp'. *Hot Rats* is regarded by many as Zappa's finest album and contains some of his very best melodic work, such as 'Peaches En Regalia', as well as some of his most inspired electric guitar

The indefatigable Frank Zappa practises his guitar licks (left), and works on a score during a plane journey (right). Zappa has frequently experimented with classical forms, and his orchestral works (below) – influenced by Varèse and Stravinsky – include six pieces which were performed by the London Symphony Orchestra in the early Eighties.

playing. The album was, furthermore, his most accessible yet, a fact reflected in its commercial success.

1970 saw Zappa involved in movies once more; his first venture was writing and directing *200 Motels*, a series of surrealistic scenes linked by the continuing story of life on the road with the Mothers. Requiring a group to play the film's music, Frank formed a new Mothers line-up that included ex-Turtles singers Mark Volman and Howard Kaylan (alias Flo and Eddie), Ian Underwood, George Duke (keyboards and trombone) and Aynsley Dunbar (drums) – but although the soundtrack music was as complex, funny and imaginative as ever, the film itself was a disappointment. Muddled and self-indulgent, *200 Motels* didn't exactly get rave reviews from the critics.

In May 1971, Frank joined John Lennon and Yoko Ono on stage at the Fillmore East and the resulting jam appeared on Lennon's *Some Time In New York City*

album. The new Mothers line-up, meanwhile, recorded *Fillmore East – June 1971* and *Just Another Band From LA*, the latter featuring one of Zappa's mini-operas, 'Billy The Mountain'. The unusual step of releasing two consecutive live albums was probably prompted by Zappa's irritation at the increasing number of live Mothers bootlegs on the market.

In the autumn of 1971, the Mothers left for a European tour which turned into a disaster: first their equipment was destroyed when the Montreux Casino in Switzerland burned down and then, in December, at a concert at London's Rainbow Theatre, Zappa was thrown from the stage by the jealous husband of one of his fans. He was seriously injured, spent weeks in hospital and the best part of a year in a wheelchair. Ever since the event he has been accompanied everywhere by a very large bodyguard and, whenever possible, has tended to avoid England.

In 1972 Zappa assembled a new team of musicians including a large number of horn players for another solo album, *Waka/Jawaka*, and enlarged the line-up with

even more horns for *The Grand Wazoo*. This was followed by *Over Nite Sensation* (1973), the first release on his new Discreet label, and *Apostrophe (')* (1974) which was his most commercial album yet – accessible and non-experimental rock music.

But by now Zappa was firmly established in the top echelon of rock performers; each year he made a world tour and released a couple of albums. This enabled him to give new material a good workout on the road, since his fans were used to being presented with mostly new material at concerts rather than the usual tired run-through of old hits. The accuracy of playing of Zappa's various line-ups and the high quality of his live recording enabled him to build up a huge volume of concert performances which were virtually indistinguishable from studio work and sections of which were often used in the montage of tapes that made up his albums. He released a lot of live material at this time: *Roxy And Elsewhere* was taken from performances during 1973-74 and *One Size Fits All* included tracks from live TV and a Helsinki concert of 1974.

1975 saw Zappa reunited with Captain Beefheart, who came out of retirement and went on the road with his old colleague. This also resulted in a live album, *Bongo Fury*, which was recorded at the Armadillo World Headquarters in Texas but never released in Britain as Virgin Records claimed to have Beefheart under contract.

The torture never stops

Throughout this period the more experimental side of Zappa's work was set to one side, possibly because he was concentrating so much on live work; instead, he provided good solid rock music with provocative lyrics and continued to develop his considerable skill as a guitarist. Then in 1976 Zappa made a move that seemed likely to mark a major commercial breakthrough when he decided to shift from his own Discreet label (distributed by Warners) to Warner Brothers itself in the hope that the company would really get behind his records and promote them.

When Warners heard *Zoot Allures*, however, they were distinctly nervous – particularly about tracks such as 'The Torture Never Stops': 10 minutes of horrible screaming, unpleasant lyrics and guitar solos that were guaranteed to stop any middle-class American dead in his tracks and make him throw up. Even worse, this was followed by 'Ms Pinky', a song about a pink sponge rubber head with a vibrator in it that Zappa found in Amsterdam. Not surprisingly, Warners didn't promote the album to Frank's satisfaction.

Zappa In New York (1978), another live LP (released on Discreet) followed, but was delayed by Warner Brothers' lawyers who were worried about the track 'Punky's Whips'. Frank began the moves to leave Warners and took to displaying a large banner at concerts reading 'Warner Bros Sucks'. Frank couldn't communicate with Warners directly due to litigation, and the label released three albums pressed from copy tapes and without line-up or recording information: *Studio Tan* (1978), *Sleep Dirt* (1979) and *Orchestral Favorites* (1979), none of which could be termed the most commercial of Frank's works. Frank then formed his own Zappa label, later changing the name to Barking Pumpkin.

Sheik Yerbouti came out in March 1979 and was composed of live tracks from London, New York and Germany. It ran into a little trouble, not from the Arab joke in its title but from the track 'Jewish Princess'. Nonetheless, it was a hit and Frank was actually nominated for two Grammy Awards. This was followed by nothing less than a full-scale rock opera, *Joe's Garage*. 'Joe's Garage is a stupid story about how the government is going to try to do away with music . . .' Zappa wrote in the sleeve notes. It had all the usual Zappa elements, including a song about nice Catholic girls turning into groupies. It was released on two albums: *Joe's Garage Act 1* and *Joe's Garage Acts 2 & 3*.

In May 1981 another live album, *Tinseltown Rebellion*, was released; this included the old favourites 'Peaches En Regalia' and 'Brown Shoes Don't Make It'. With his own label, Zappa was able to release anything that he wanted and did so: three albums of guitar solos, later issued as a boxed set called *Shut Up And Play Yer Guitar*.

Beyond the valley . . .

You Are What You Is followed in 1981 and *Ship Arriving Too Late To Save A Drowning Witch* (named after the cover drawing) in 1982. The latter contained the minor hit single 'Valley Girl', which was described by Zappa as 'another in a long series of songs about who does what to whom'. He began work on a TV show based on the song and also negotiated merchandising rights for Valley Girl dolls and artefacts.

Zappa announced that he would not tour Europe again because of the rising costs and growing violence at his concerts. He did, however, visit England in 1982 to supervise the recording of six of his orchestral pieces by the 100-strong London Symphony Orchestra, who also performed the pieces at the Barbican Centre.

Zappa spent more of the Eighties reissuing his back catalogue on compact disc than producing new product. The major work, *You Can't Do That On Stage Anymore,* was a 12-CD set of live recordings from 1969 to 1984—a staggering 13 hours of music.

"I don't care if I'm known or remembered, respected or get famous," the seemingly tireless Zappa has commented. "The reason I write music is because I like people to listen to it, and if there are other people who like to listen to it then that's fine." MILES

Right: Zappa pauses to contemplate his next move. Inset above right: Flo and Eddie, alias Mark Volman and Howard Kaylan of the Turtles, joined the Mothers in 1970.

FRANK ZAPPA
Discography to 1982

Singles
How Could I Be Such A Fool/Help I'm A Rock (Verve 10418, 1966); How Could I Be Such A Fool/It Can't Happen Here (Verve 10418, 1966); Who Are The Brain Police/Trouble Comin' Every Day (Verve 10458, 1966); Motherly Love/I Ain't Got No Heart (Verve DV 5012, 1966); Big Leg Emma/Why Don't You Do Me Right (Verve 10513, 1967); Mother People/Lonely Little Girl (Verve 10570, 1967); Jelly Roll Gum Drop/Deseri (Verve 10632, 1968); Any Way The Wind Blows/Jelly Roll Gum Drop (Verve 10632, 1968); My Guitar/Dog Breath (Bizarre 0840, 1969); Peaches En Regalia/Little Umbrellas (Bizarre 0889, 1970); WPLJ/My Guitar (Bizarre 0892, 1970); Tell Me You Love Me/Would You Go All The Way . . . (Bizarre 0967, 1970); Magic Fingers/Daddy, Daddy, Daddy (United Artists 50857, 1971); Tears Began To Fall/Junier Mintz Boogie (Bizarre 1052, 1971); Cletus Awreetus Awrightus/Eat That Question (Bizarre 1127, 1972); I'm The Slime/Montana (Discreet 1180, 1973); Don't Eat The Yellow Snow/Cosmic Debris (Discreet 1312, 1974); Find Her Finer/Zoot Allures (Warner Bros 8926, 1976); Disco Boy/Ms. Pinky (Warner Bros 8342, 1976); Dancin' Fool/Baby Snakes (Zappa Z-10, 1979); Joe's Garage/Central Scrutinizer (Zappa Z-31, 1979); I Don't Wanna Get Drafted/Ancient Armaments (Zappa ZR 1001, 1980); Goblin Girl/Pink Napkins (Barking Pumpkin W99 02616, 1981); You Are What You Is/Harder Than Your Husband (Barking Pumpkin W99 02936, 1981); Valley Girl/You Are What You Is (Barking Pumpkin 4W9 03069, 1982).

Albums
Freak Out (Verve V6 5005, 1966); *Absolutely Free* (Verve V6 5013, 1967); *We're Only In It For The Money* (Verve V6 5045, 1968); *Lumpy Gravy* (Verve V6 8741, 1968); *Cruisin' With Ruben And The Jets* (Verve V6 5055, 1968); *Mothermania* (Verve V6 8741, 1968); *Uncle Meat* (Bizarre MS 2024, 1969); *Hot Rats* (Bizarre RS RS 6356, 1969); *Burnt Weenie Sandwich* (Bizarre RS 6370, 1969); *Weasels Ripped My Flesh* (Bizarre MS 2028, 1970); *Chunga's Revenge* (Bizarre MS 2030, 1970); *Fillmore East – June 1971* (Bizarre MS 2042, 1971); *200 Motels* (United Artists UAS 9956, 1971); *Just Another Band From LA* (Bizarre MS 2075, 1972); *Waka/Jawaka* (Bizarre MS 2094, 1972); *The Grand Wazoo* (Bizarre MS 2093, 1972); *Over Nite Sensation* (Discreet MS 2149, 1973); *Apostrophe(')* (Discreet DS 2175, 1974); *Roxy And Elsewhere* (Discreet DS 2202, 1974); *One Size Fits All* (Discreet DS 2216, 1975); *Bongo Fury* (Discreet DS 2234, 1975); *Zoot Allures* (Warner Bros BS 2970, 1976); *Zappa In New York* (Discreet 2D 2290, 1978); *Studio Tan* (Discreet DSK 2291, 1978); *Sleep Dirt* (Discreet DSK 2292, 1979); *Sheik Yerbouti* (Zappa SRZ 2-1501, 1979); *Orchestral Favorites* (Discreet DSK 2294, 1979); *Joe's Garage Act I* (Zappa SRZ 1-1603, 1979); *Joe's Garage Acts II & III* (Zappa SRZ 2-1502, 1979); *Tinsel Town Rebellion* (Barking Pumpkin PW 2-37336, 1981); *Shut Up 'N Play Yer Guitar* (Barking Pumpkin BPR 1111, 1981); *Shut Up 'N Play Yer Guitar Some More* (Barking Pumpkin BPR 1112, 1981); *Return Of The Son Of Shut Up 'N Play Yer Guitar* (Barking Pumpkin BPR 1113, 1981); *You Are What You Is* (Barking Pumpkin PW 2-37537, 1981); *Ship Arriving Too Late To Save A Drowning Witch* (Barking Pumpkin 1114, 1982).

RAW POWER

Above: Iggy Pop bends over backwards to entertain his audience with his violent, bizarre and scandalous stage act.

Psychedelic Stooges in 1967. The group comprised Iggy on vocals, Ron Asheton on lead guitar, Dave Alexander on bass and Ron's brother Scott on drums. Legend has it that the group made their debut on Halloween night 1968 in Iggy's old home town of Ann Arbor.

Over the next two years the Stooges built up a reputation as the dumbest, nastiest, most outrageous live act ever to have charmed their way into the hearts of the Midwest of America. As a stage performer, Iggy took everything to excess and then doubled it. A Stooges performance demanded audience participation. Iggy would taunt and bait audiences to a frenzy and then pull one of his bravura stunts: hurling himself into the audience to beat or be beaten (usually the latter); shredding his chest with a broken beer bottle; vomiting; engaging in oral sex with members of the audience; being carried aloft on the upraised hands of his fans.

Elektra Records came, saw and were sufficiently impressed at this display of Dionysian excess to sign up the Stooges (along with fellow Detroit retards the MC5). The result was a 1969 debut LP, called *The Stooges* and produced by John Cale, fresh from his experiences with the Velvet Underground. The first verse of the first track, '1969', summed up the mood of the record perfectly: 'It's 1969 OK/All across the USA/It's another year for me and you/Another year with nothing to do.' The tracks alternated between brutal exorcisms of frustration, such as 'No Fun', later (perhaps inevitably) performed by the Sex Pistols, and celebrations of unholy lust, as in 'I Wanna Be Your Dog'.

Nasty Pop

The group struggled through various personnel changes, though retaining the core of Iggy and the Asheton brothers, and completed a second album, *Fun House*, for Elektra in 1970. Produced by Don Gallucci, it was basically the same mixture as before – but Iggy did enhance his reputation with the inclusion of that masterpiece of paranoia, 'TV Eye', while saxophone added a touch of sophistication to the album. The generous hints of manic depravity on *Fun House* proved more symptomatic of the group's state, however, and the Stooges – by this time including ex-Chosen Few member James Williamson on rhythm guitar – fell apart in 1971 as a result of one drug frenzy too many.

Salvation arrived from an unexpected source. David Bowie and his manager Tony DeFries brought Pop and Williamson to London, wired airfares to the Asheton brothers to join them, and put the reformed Stooges in the studio. With Bowie masterminding the final mix, Williamson co-writing all the songs and providing lead guitar, Ron Asheton demoted to bass and Iggy revitalised, *Raw Power*, released on CBS in 1973, proved to be the Stooges'

The primal punk-rock of Iggy and the Stooges

'I'VE BEEN THROUGH IT ALL. I've been the puppet, the arsehole, the dupe, the junkie and I've come through it and proved I'm the equal to anybody you'd care to mention.' Thus spake Iggy Pop – and if the mere fact of survival confers status, there's no contradicting him. As it happens, there is also the bonus of a series of some of the most enjoyably demented rock'n'roll performances ever to (dis)grace stage or vinyl. A baby-face perched on top of one of the most impressive torsos in the profession, Iggy Pop is by turn petulant, strident, malevolent and repentant – a perfect specimen of the rock regressive.

James Jewel Osterburg was born on 21 April 1947 in Ann Arbor, Michigan, a town just to the west of the great US motor city of Detroit. His parents were both school-teachers and his teens were outwardly unremarkable, although Iggy later commented: 'I was unhappy and self-conscious when young. When I was about 18 I was really loony, got into a series of tremendous car accidents, unbelievable ones where everybody else got killed and I never got scratched. That was the first time in my life I ever felt anything like it – such power and such timelessness.'

Fortunately for Iggy, the second time he felt the power was when he played in a rock'n'roll group – the Iguanas – in which he was both drummer and lead singer. He left to join local rivals the Prime Movers, a blues band, before drifting to Chicago's South Side to play with Sam Lay, the original drummer in Paul Butterfield's Blues Band. Having gained a new name from his first group (Iggy) and a warped blues vision from his subsequent wanderings, he went to Detroit and got down to real business with the formation of the finest hour. However, neither the modest success of the album in America nor Bowie and DeFries' MainMan organisation could save the Stooges from their baser instincts, and by the end of 1974 they had split.

The last will and testament appeared in 1976 with the release on Skydog Records of *Metallic KO*, a (very bad) recording of the group's last-ever gig at Detroit's Michigan Palace. The record is subtitled 'Open Up And Bleed', which is apt enough as on the second side of the LP Iggy taunts the audience unmercifully through a trio of 'songs' – 'Rich Bitch', 'Cock In My Pocket' and an X-rated version of 'Louie Louie' – until the persistent shower of bottles and glasses ends the fun.

Iggy Pop retired to the West Coast after the split, recording occasionally and indulging his taste for drugs. Some of the music recorded during this period subsequently appeared on a 1978 album *Kill City*, produced by James Williamson. Considering its haphazard genesis, it is a remarkably coherent achievement, and it also contains one of Iggy's finest love songs in 'Johanna'.

Idiot reflections

Having cleaned up in hospital in Los Angeles, Iggy teamed up again with long-suffering fan/mentor David Bowie in 1977 to produce two of his most powerful records on RCA. The first of this pair, *The Idiot*, represented something of a catharsis, with Iggy spitting out the bitter dregs of his past experiences in a series of tracks that included the sinister 'Sister Midnight' and a classic of hollow fun, 'Nightclubbing'. He even found time for an elegy to the Stooges in 'Dum Dum Boys'. *Lust For Life* followed quickly and, as its title indicates, represented a return to the artist as barnstormer; the sleazy swing of 'The Passenger' and the manic verve of 'Some Weird Sin' and the title track were joined by a couple of numbers in which Iggy displayed an unhealthy obsession with people turning blue to provide Pop's second great vinyl moment (after *Raw Power*).

It was entirely characteristic of Iggy Pop that, at the very moment when every other lame-brained UK punk outfit was parading the exhumed carcass of one of his early Stooges classics in its set, he chose to forge ahead with a new brand of electronic rock that possessed a range breathtaking in comparison. Iggy reacted angrily to his new status as 'The Godfather of Punk': 'Some people think that the music I make is just some sort of violence/stomp thing and that everyone who made it before me is dead and most of the ones that made it after me are unemployed.'

The delicate balance of this harmonious relationship was not maintained, however. After wrapping up his RCA contract with the delivery of the somewhat anti-climac-

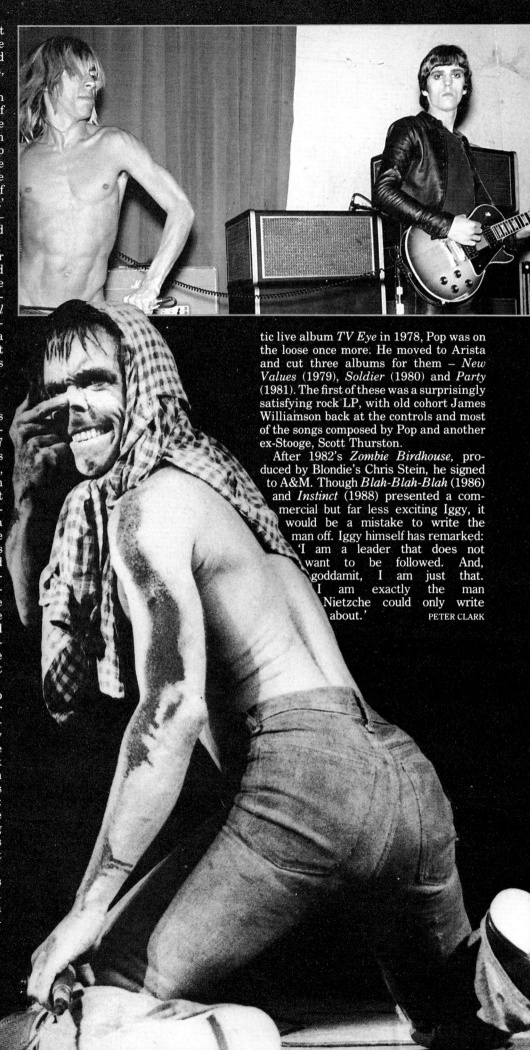

tic live album *TV Eye* in 1978, Pop was on the loose once more. He moved to Arista and cut three albums for them – *New Values* (1979), *Soldier* (1980) and *Party* (1981). The first of these was a surprisingly satisfying rock LP, with old cohort James Williamson back at the controls and most of the songs composed by Pop and another ex-Stooge, Scott Thurston.

After 1982's *Zombie Birdhouse*, produced by Blondie's Chris Stein, he signed to A&M. Though *Blah-Blah-Blah* (1986) and *Instinct* (1988) presented a commercial but far less exciting Iggy, it would be a mistake to write the man off. Iggy himself has remarked: 'I am a leader that does not want to be followed. And, goddamit, I am just that. I am exactly the man Nietzche could only write about.'   PETER CLARK

Above left: Pop rocks London's Roxy club, 1977. Above right: On stage with cohort James Williamson on guitar. Right: A characteristic Iggy pose.

Above and insets: The chief Stooge displays his well-maintained torso and characteristic lust for live performance with all the snarling animal energy for which he is famed.

Iggy Pop
Recommended Listening

Fun House (Elektra K42032) (Includes: Down On The Street, TV Eye, Dirt, 1970, Fun House, LA Blues, Loose); *Lust For Life* (RCA PL12275) (Includes: Success, The Passenger, Some Weird Sin, Lust For Life, Turn Blue, Tonight).

Gonna Make You a Star

Manufacturing pop idols became a moneyspinning industry

THE STORY OF ROCK has been as much a tale of record companies in search of profits as one of musical integrity and virtuosity. From the Fifties, rock music has generated massive profits for record companies, publishing houses, booking agencies, managers, producers, session musicians and, finally, the recording artists themselves.

The creation and definition of pop stars has its antecedents in Hollywood. Movies provided (and still provide) stereotypes that could be easily recognised and understood by the public – the precocious kid, the boy-and-girl-next-door, the teenage rebel, the Latin heart-throb, the tough guy or the curvaceous sex symbol. All these have been adopted by the music business. As with the selling of movies, soapflakes or motor cars, sex has always been a main selling-point in the industry's marketing of its product.

The most direct and pernicious forms of market manipulation concern the bribing of disc jockeys to play certain records (payola) and the practice of 'hyping' records into the charts. Rather more legitimate attempts to manipulate the popular music market may be divided into two main phases: the years up until the

David Cassidy (top) and Donny Osmond (above) were both sold as clean-living American boys-next-door, each the perfect son, brother or boyfriend. But puppy love couldn't last, and after 1972-73 their millions of fans moved on to new idols.

mid-Sixties, when the major companies had little understanding of the market's workings, and were outpaced by the enterprise of those running independent record labels; and the years since then, when a generation brought up on rock, with an intuitive understanding of the basic precepts of rock'n'roll and its audience, achieved corporate influence.

Assembly-line stars

The packaging of rock singers or groups is a conservative reaction to the fluctuations of an uncertain market. The basic presupposition is that a potential market exists and that it can be reached merely through the presentation of the right set of ingredients. Groups produced in this way signal the industry's occasional bafflement with its audience and its hopeful attempts to prove that the music business abides by the same rules as any other: that logical reasons govern purchase, rather than merely emotional response.

Exposure is crucial to the creation of new stars. One way of achieving this is to have them appear regularly on television shows. In the late Fifties, the record companies around

Philadelphia were quick to adopt this policy, using Dick Clark's 'American Bandstand' as a means of exposing their acts to the television audience.

When manufactured artists are conceived and marketed correctly, large profits can result. During the mid Sixties, American media companies saw the commercial possibilities of fabricating a group and then showcasing it in a television series: the result was the Monkees, created by NBC-TV in 1966 to be America's instant answer to the Beatles.

The popularity of the Monkees led to further experimentation in this area with 'The Archies' and 'The Partridge Family' series, both aimed at the same teenybop audience so unerringly exploited by the Monkees. The Archies were simply a group of session singers backing cartoon characters, and the limitations of this idea resulted in only one hit, 'Sugar Sugar'. 'The Partridge Family' format, however, was much better realised. The shows were a nice blend of cosy family security and pop, featuring a trendy young mum (Shirley Jones) and her attractive singing family. Its success was instrumental in launching David Cassidy as an international heart-throb in the early Seventies.

'The Partridge Family' showed the way for other family acts like the Osmonds. The teenies were thus granted stars of their own tender years to worship, as first Donny (with 'Puppy Love') and then Little Jimmy Osmond (with 'Long Haired Lover From Liverpool') stormed the charts.

Sound and vision
The British music industry did not have such ready access to television as its American counterpart, lacking the latter's multi-media interests and involvements. While the BBC and ITV networks featured established acts on such shows as 'Thank Your Lucky Stars', 'Ready, Steady, Go!' and 'Top Of The Pops', the stations themselves initially lacked either the commercial initiative or the funds to originate their own series based around a 'manufactured' group. The chart popularity of theme tunes or songs from television programmes created no new stars, being performed by established artists. Apart from the launching of Sheena Easton via the BBC's 'The Big Time' series and the showing of the American series 'Fame'

(which prompted a run of hit LPs, singles and live tours in Britain), for many years the utilisation of television by the British record industry was best exemplified by the groups representing the United Kingdom in the Eurovision Song Contest.

Bucks Fizz were just such a group. Brought together to perform 'Making Your Mind Up' for the 1981 contest, they went on to gain a rapid succession of chart hits. As much as any of the aforementioned American stars, Bucks Fizz sell a carefully constructed image – that of fun-loving (though also knowingly sexy) boys-and-girls-next-door.

From the Seventies onwards the use of video promotional films has revolutionised the marketing of an artist's product. No longer content with showing their acts simply miming on stage on television shows, record companies both in Britain and the US have invested huge sums to ensure their bands have maximum visual appeal, employing first-rate directors, such as Don Letts and Steve Barron.

The Svengalis of swing
With television initially playing only a minor role in the marketing of new acts, the British record industry preferred to pick up on reliable indicators of market potential, usually through the prior existence of an act having a strong local following. When musical trends moved too fast for the music companies to keep pace, market manipulation fell into the hands of entrepreneurs who located a market need, found a product to fill it and only then involved the record industry.

In the Fifties, the British music business had been thrown into disarray by the rock'n'roll boom. Hitherto attuned to crooners and dance bands, it attempted to meet the American invasion with homegrown acts, but had no idea where challengers could be found. Reliance was thus placed on businessmen such as Larry Parnes who claimed to understand the new style. Potential stars were discovered, given unlikely names like Marty Wilde and Billy Fury, and touted around the variety circuit (then the British record industry's equivalent to television). The story of Tommy Steele's success was a prime example of his commercial skill; Parnes plucked a semi-pro singer, Thomas Hicks, from obscurity and moulded him, somewhat spuriously, into the first

Above left: David Essex, a pop star who graduated from stage and screen, answers his fan mail. Perfecting a homely blend of cockney charm and unthreatening sex appeal, dishy David continued to make hearts flutter through the Seventies and Eighties. Above: 'Fame', an American TV series based on Alan Parker's 1980 film, promised showbiz success for aspiring young dancers – and captivated millions of youthful viewers, particularly in the UK. Spin-off records and tours made The Kids From Fame *industry an especially productive one.*

indigenous rock'n'roll star.

Parnes' achievements were mirrored in the Seventies and Eighties by Malcolm McLaren – both men constructed a myth that they alone understood the new music fashions. With the Sex Pistols and, later, Bow Wow Wow, McLaren (who in 1982 became a pop star himself with his single 'Buffalo Gals') crystallised images and musical styles intended deliberately to shock accepted standards and gain publicity for group and manager. His methods and his protégés' anarchic exploits – documented in the Sex Pistols' film *The Great Rock 'n'Roll Swindle* (1980) – temporarily rocked the major companies, who were suddenly made aware of how pitifully out of touch they were.

Managers or producers often effect dramatic changes in an act's image; these transformations are the stuff of rock mythology, seemingly magic tales of the changing of water into wine. The Beatles and the Rolling Stones, who first achieved fame under the guidance of astute managers, are often cited as examples of this 'mythical' process, although this view tends to demean the raw materials with which Brian Epstein and Andrew Loog Oldham respectively worked. Neither created the group, but both concentrated on refining its appearance and public image. The two men rechannelled pre-existing talent using their own business acumen and contacts. They gave the impression that the rock market worked logically after all.

In their assessment of how to get an act noticed, both followed in the footsteps of Alan Freed. Freed offered advice and help about the best way for early rock'n'roll singers to hit the big time, often for a percentage of the profits. He successfully contrived to present black music to a white audience; under these conditions, acts needed advice on what songs and what clothes were suitable for the new market.

A similar case was that of Elvis Presley and his manager Colonel Tom Parker. Parker himself always maintained that the music was Presley's business but that the packaging of it was his own. That marketing was concerned with the public face of the performer and the ways in which it could be used to generate the consumption of product. Elvis made the music, Parker made sure it sold.

Here come the mirror men

The most daring metamorphoses of all are often those brought about by the artists themselves. By changing his image, a singer automatically hopes to associate himself with another, potentially more fruitful market. Such changes sometimes go beyond the mere following of fashion: David Bowie's continual repackaging of himself, from Mod to the androgynous Ziggy Stardust, to the soul boy of 'Young Americans', to the mime of 'Ashes To Ashes', is the prime example of a recording artist continually redefining his audience. By repeatedly altering his persona, Bowie both anticipates and follows fashion, bringing the style of the avant-garde to the marketplace in a saleable form.

The radical changes undergone by Bowie have not been matched by any other performer, though the principle of searching for new and more attractive markets has long been an accepted one. Other image changes have involved moves towards a commercial market from the underground, as was the case with Marc Bolan, or have been the result of a chance hit, as was the case with Gary Glitter, where the surprise success was sustained by the star's flair for self-publicity.

It is a showbusiness truism that, once out of favour, it is hard to make a comeback. Year after year the public makes clear that it just isn't interested in repackaged versions of old favourites – witness the problems of David Cassidy in gaining acceptance as an artist after the waves of teen hysteria had abated. Novelty plays an important part in the selling process, as bands like the Goombay Dance Band, Tight Fit and the Wombles have shown, but in the long run an act must have more than just a cleverly constructed image to survive for long in the jungle of the music industry.   PAUL FRYER

Below: Tight Fit – alias 'Tarzan' Steve Grant and his two 'Janes', brunette Denise Gyngell and blonde Julie Harris – was a group manufactured and marketed as three bodies beautiful and, with the help of a jokey studio-jungle video, their version of 'The Lion Sleeps Tonight' topped the UK charts in 1982. But later the girls were sacked, being replaced by two near-identical pop starlets.

Puppy Love

The wholesome appeal of the Osmond family

'IT WAS NOT UNTIL groups like the Osmond brothers appeared on the scene that the pop revolution really got underway,' wrote Richard Robinson in his 1972 book *The Osmond Brothers And The New Pop Scene.* 'Ignoring the psychedelic effects and spaced-out rock and roll that has been so popular during the past five years, the Osmonds started a whole new musical era with their refreshing, exciting sounds.' This, of course, was patent nonsense: rather than offering anything new, the Osmonds represented a return to the pre-Beatles teen-idol traditions of Philadelphia.

Of all the teen-pop stars to emerge in the early Seventies, the Osmonds were the cleanest, the most wholesome and respectable. Unlike Marc Bolan, they didn't pout sexily; unlike Sweet, they didn't don effeminate make-up; unlike David Cassidy, they didn't wiggle bottoms suggestively; unlike the Jackson Five, they weren't black. Like the Avalons, Rydells and Fabians of the previous decade, the Osmond brothers were tame, safe and conservative; and, with few to rival their smiling, unthreatening approach, their brief but enormous commercial success far outstripped that of the Sixties Philly teen idols from whom they borrowed so much.

With seven singing siblings, the Osmond family were able to penetrate more than just one corner of the market. For the teens, there was a five-piece group who provided uptempo pop; for the pre-pubescents, there was the group's principal star Donny with his solo ballads of forbidden teenage romance (all, incidentally, revivals of hits by such boys-next-door of yesteryear as Paul Anka, Frankie Avalon and Tab Hunter); for tots and their grandparents there were the bouncy, chirruping novelties of the podgy, pre-teen Little Jimmy; and for middle-aged lovers of middle-of-the-road country fare, there was sister Marie, alone or duetting with Donny. The Osmond family had it made.

Family favourites

Olive and George Osmond were a strict Mormon couple from Salt Lake City, Utah, who had eight sons and a daughter. The two eldest, Virl and Tom, were born partially deaf, but the next four arrivals, Alan (born 22 June 1949), Wayne (28 August 1951), Merrill (30 April 1953) and Jay (2 March 1955), were perfect specimens who quickly learned the art of close harmony singing from their father and saxophone-playing mother. At family gatherings, the four brothers developed a barbershop act and were soon performing songs like 'The Old Oaken Bucket' at Mormon church functions.

On holiday in California in 1961, the boys visited Disneyland, were invited on stage to sing and, as a result, were offered a

Below: George and Olive Osmond pose proudly among their singing brood.

residency at the amusement centre. Here, they were spotted one night by the father of Andy Williams, who recommended the youthful quartet to his singing-star son. The Osmond brothers were booked to appear on 'The Andy Williams Show' and were subsequently given a regular spot on the programme. Further television work followed: the boys acted in 'The Travels Of Jamie McPheeters', a Western adventure series starring Charles Bronson and a young Kurt Russell; they sang on 'The Jerry Lewis Show' and guested in a TV special, 'The Seven Little Foys', which marked the arrival of five-year-old kid brother Donny (born 9 December 1957).

The Osmonds continued to perform variety acts on stage and TV throughout the Sixties, singing old-time melodies and tap-dancing. Then, in 1970, the Jackson Five hit the US singles charts with 'ABC'. The sudden popularity of five brothers – the youngest of whom, Michael, was the same age as Donny – did not escape the attention of George and Olive Osmond. Their offspring were offered to MGM Records as a white alternative to the Jacksons – MGM recognised the possibilities and dispatched the boys to Muscle Shoals studios to record a single. Written by George Jackson, 'One Bad Apple' was a virtual copy of the Jackson Five's sound – Donny's exuberant falsetto emulating that of Michael Jackson – and in February 1971, the record reached the top of the American charts.

Further success followed with 'Double Lovin'' and Joe South's 'Yo-Yo', and by the beginning of 1972, the Osmonds had taken over from the Jacksons and David Cassidy as the most adored pin-ups of teen-magazine subscribers. As if to underline the fact, ABC-TV had replaced their cartoon series 'The Jackson Five' with one called 'The Osmonds', consisting of scrappily-animated stories in which the boys were 'appointed goodwill ambassadors by the United States Music Commitee' and got into all sorts of scrapes.

It was apparent from the start that the appeal of the Osmonds was based largely on Donny's boyish innocence. He was hardly stunningly good-looking – like his brothers, he had a pudgy face, a snub-nose and over-large teeth – but little girls doted on him nonetheless and, while the Osmonds continued producing hits as a group, Donny pursued a parallel solo career as a juvenile, teen-throb balladeer.

In June 1972, his third solo single 'Puppy Love' (which had reached Number 3 in the US earlier in the year) made the top of the British charts.

In October, the Osmonds arrived at London's Heathrow Airport to find 8000 young girls waiting and screaming. The group's visit had been preceded by a massive media build-up, and British TV, press and radio seemed anxious to get as much mileage out of the family as possible. In the following weeks, the airwaves and papers were dominated by the sight and sound of the toothy teen idols. The brothers' public

Right: A bemused pair of policemen protect teen-throb balladeer Donny Osmond from over-excited fans.
Above: The Osmond brothers execute a slick stage routine.

persona was inoffensive and predictable to the point of nausea. Interviews with Donny were always the same – he loved girls but was too young to date – while his older brothers were forever uttering platitudes like: 'If we can make people happy with our music, that's great.'

Whatever they recorded, British teenagers bought, and for the next two years the family members, in their various You' and Tommy Edwards' 'Morning Side Of The Mountain', while the Osmonds as a whole achieved their first UK Number 1 with the smooth 'Love Me For A Reason'.

By the end of 1974, however, the Osmonds' popularity was declining rapid-

Sibilant siblings Marie and Donny Osmond notched four UK Top Thirty hits as a duo.

throughout the Sixties: while children turned their fantasy-attentions to other singing stars, middle-aged Americans tuned in to Donny and Marie's TV series, applauded the singing, dancing Osmonds in Atlantic City casinos, followed Marie's on-off marriage saga in *People* magazine and were sold exotic fruit juice by brother and sister trilling jingles on tropical beaches during commercial breaks.

permutations, churned out hits. On 9 December 1972, the group reached Number 2 with their lightweight rocker 'Crazy Horses' (a protest against automobile pollution written by Alan and Merrill) while two weeks later the overweight and precocious nine-year-old Little Jimmy Osmond (born 16 April 1963) made the top with the music-hall chirpiness of 'Long Haired Lover From Liverpool'. In 1973, Donny hit the top twice with 'The Twelfth Of Never' and 'Young Love', while sister Marie (born 13 October 1959) made Number 2 with Anita Bryant's 1960 C&W hit 'Paper Roses'. The following year, Donny and Marie teamed up for Top Ten versions of Dale and Grace's 'I'm Leaving It Up To

ly. Donny was growing up and so were his fans, while the group's image of untarnished, grinning wholesomeness had become irritating. Their attempt at rock credibility with *The Plan* (1973), an album entirely written, played and produced by the group, had failed miserably – the musical performance was competent enough but the material itself was mediocre, while the record's religious 'concept' was hardly likely to seduce a rock audience.

In 1975, while the even less gifted and charismatic Bay City Rollers took charge of the British teen-pop market, the Osmonds were virtually forgotten. The family now returned to the type of audience that had sustained them

Although the Osmond family no longer sold records, mother Olive had invested her children's earnings wisely, building up a multi-million dollar record and publishing business and marketing cassette tapes of *The Story Of Joseph Smith* (the founder of Mormonism). The clan that *Life* magazine had once described as 'a plague of wholesomeness' would never starve.

TOM HIBBERT

The Osmonds
Recommended Listening

Live (MGM Super 2315 117) (Includes: Down By The Lazy River, Yo-Yo, One Bad Apple, Sometimes I Feel Like A Motherless Child, Your Song, Hey Girl, Free).

ROCK ON

David Essex: acting the teen idol

IF YOU HAD GONE to a David Essex concert in the mid Seventies, you would have found yourself surrounded by screaming pre-pubescent girls. Not only did their repeated cries of 'David' make it extremely difficult to hear any of his songs, but the danger of a stampede for the stage posed a very real threat not only to the fans themselves but also to the object of their reverence. David Essex, though, had his own way to deal with this. Whereas other teenybopper stars like T.Rex, Mud, David Cassidy, Gary Glitter, the Sweet and Alvin

Stardust had their shows disturbed in this way, Essex announced that if there were any storming of the stage, the music would stop. Although his early success rested on his boyish good looks and teen appeal, he was firmly committed to his music and its theatrical content. This, more than anything, has been the reason for his continued success.

From Hell's Kitchen to Godspell

Although it might have seemed to an outsider that David Essex had burst onto the scene overnight as Jesus in *Godspell* in 1971, this was far from the case. Born David Albert Cook in Plaistow, East London on 23 July 1947, he grew up in the

Above: The tousled, boy-next-door looks of David Essex – was this the face that launched a thousand fainting fits?

Hell's Kitchen area of London's docklands, a tough area at the best of times. He quickly learned that, to survive, he had to join one of the local gangs. But he also realized he had to make it on his own: 'I began to think like a lot of kids around the area – that you've got to grab it, because no-one's going to give it to you.'

By the age of 13, he was playing truant from school to work in the local street market; within a year or so, he brushed with the law for riding a borrowed motorcycle under age. His obsession with bikes –

echoed in 1980 in his film *Silver Dream Racer* – had started, and his obsession with music was shortly to follow.

After his first taste of R&B at the Flamingo Club in Wardour Street, he persuaded his father to spend some money on a second-hand drum kit. He joined his first group – the Everons, a semi-pro blues band – in 1963 and, with stardom in mind, gave up his apprenticeship as an engineer. Life as a musician was not to be easy, however, and over the next seven years his 10 singles all flopped. Manager Derek Bowman, who had seen him in those very early days and believed in his boy, did not give up. He moved his charge sideways into repertory theatre, with a lead part in a musical called *The Fantasticks*. In this and other productions up and down the country, David Essex gained invaluable acting experience. He even had bit parts in two films – *Assault* (1970) and *All Coppers Are* (1971) – but his break was to come at the end of 1971 when he was cast, out of 6000 applicants, to play Jesus in *Godspell*. The musical opened at the Roundhouse but quickly transferred to Wyndham's in the West End, where he played the part for two years.

Taking time out from *Godspell*, he co-starred with Ringo Starr in the film *That'll Be The Day* (1973), an evocative look at late Fifties youth culture and clumsy adolescent sexuality. David played Jim Maclaine, a working-class kid trying to be a star, a part that could have been written for Essex. The film ends with hints of hopes to come; but David was soon to surpass his fictional *alter ego*, achieving the stardom that Jim Maclaine sought.

Stardust

'Rock On', written by David Essex for the film, became his first hit, entering the UK charts in September 1973 where it remained for eight weeks, selling 3 million copies and peaking at Number 3. 'Lamplight' followed two months later, reaching Number 7, followed by 'America', all tracks from his first LP *Rock On*. His second LP, simply entitled *David Essex* (1974), yielded the hit single 'Gonna Make You A Star', which stayed in the charts for 12 weeks, reaching Number 1 in the UK and Number 3 in the States. This album also spawned his next hit – 'Stardust' – which hit the charts in December 1974 and reached Number 7; it was also the title of his next film, released in the same year.

Made as a sequel to *That'll Be The Day*, *Stardust* co-starred Adam Faith and Larry Hagman. It depicted Jim Maclaine's reactions to stardom; in the course of the film, he loses touch with his group, his audience and eventually with reality, overdosing on drugs. Unlike the character

Right: Essex on stage in the early Eighties, when his shows comprised a mix of his own hits and rock'n'roll standards. Far right: With Paul Nicholas in Stardust. *Essex gave a commanding performance as an idealistic, egotistical rock star.*

he portrayed, however, David Essex didn't succumb to the pressures of the music industry, but managed to keep his feet on the ground and remain in control of his own career. While glitter and glam-rock were in fashion, he would sport ordinary and even 'jumble sale' clothes, as he was depicted in 1975 on the cover of his third album, *All The Fun Of The Fair*.

His first six albums showed a lively song-writing talent. They include over 50 songs of his own composition. Of these 'Rolling Stone', 'If I Could', 'City Lights' and 'Coming Home' were all smash hits, and 'Hold Me Close' repeated the chart success of 'Gonna Make You A Star'. He drew extensively on his own experiences in his songs – 'If I Could', for example, was about the tough East End of London—and he could write a hard-rock number just as effectively as a sentimental ballad.

Following *Godspell* and the two hit films, he began the rounds of numerous TV shows, undertook sell-out tours of Australia and the US and recorded the albums *Out On The Street* (1976) and *Gold And Ivory* (1977), both of which he produced himself. His love of the stage, however, was never far away and in 1978 he returned to the West End to portray Che Guevara in the Tim Rice/Andrew Lloyd-Webber musical *Evita*. With this went a change of record label, from CBS to Phonogram and another hit single 'Oh, What A Circus', a song taken from the show.

Evita was followed by another tour, the albums *Imperial Wizard* (1979) and *Hot Love* (1980), and another film, *Silver Dream Racer*, for which he wrote the score; the title song was a Number 3 hit single. His 1981 LP *Be-Bop The Future* was produced by Al Kooper and featured such prestigious musicians as Steely Dan's Jeff Baxter, Herbie Flowers, John 'Rabbit' Bundrick and Kooper himself. That year David Essex again returned to the West End theatre, this time for a straight role as Lord Byron in Romulus Winney's 'Childe Byron' at the Young Vic.

An embarrassing TV appearance as a singing MC on 'The David Essex Showcase' series was redeemed in 1982 by two huge hits – 'Me And My Girl (Nightclubbing)' and 'A Winter's Tale'. The latter was a throwback to *Godspell* and *Evita* in that the lyrics were penned by Tim Rice; music was by Mike Batt.

By the late Eighties, he could look back on a moderately successful stage show *Mutiny On The Bounty,* a 1986 TV-advertised album of stage favourites and a small-screen debut in BBC's *The River* (1988) that boded well for the future. Essex's willingness to work and diversify must be a secret of his continuing success.

JOHN STRETTON

David Essex
Recommended Listening

The David Essex Album (CBS 1101) (Includes: Gonna Make You A Star, Lamplight, Hold Me Close, Rock On, Stardust, America).

ROLLERMANIA!

During 1974 and 1975, the Bay City Rollers were the teen sensation of Britain. At the peak of their popularity, their fan club claimed to be receiving 11,000 letters a *day*, and they were selling millions of records around the world. They scored ten Top Ten hits in Britain and reached Number 1 in America. They also split the pop world in two. Their hysterical adolescent fans treated them as gods, but to nearly everyone else they were simply five rather dim Scots boys in half-mast trousers and tartan scarfs.

The Bay City Rollers started life as the Saxons, an Edinburgh band formed by the school-age Longmuir brothers Alan (born 20 June 1953) and Derek (born 19 March

From Scotland came the tartan tearaways . . .

1952). Their first break came early in 1969 when Alan eventually persuaded local dance band leader Tam Paton to come and listen to them. Tired of having his coffee breaks at the Palais de Danse interrupted by this strangely persistent 15-year-old, Paton finally went along just to get the boy off his back. The group's music wasn't up to much – the usual schoolboy versions of Beatles songs played in the back bedroom of an Edinburgh council flat – but their enthusiasm convinced Paton that he should take them on. At this stage they

had played only a few local gigs, first as the Saxons and then the Bay City Rollers, but Paton, who had no previous managerial experience, managed to get them a residency at the local Top Storey club and dressed them in pink suits and black bow ties.

Edinburgh rock
He also gave up his own musical career and worked instead as a lorry driver with his father's wholesale business so he could devote more time to the group. The Rollers spent the next two years playing around Scotland, gathering a large following but making little money. Then in 1971 Dick Leahy, head of Bell Records in the UK,

found himself with a few hours to kill in Edinburgh after missing a plane home and was persuaded to see the group. The frenzied teenage reaction to the Rollers' bouncy pop tunes so amazed Leahy that he decided to sign them up.

The group now consisted of Derek (drums), Alan (bass), Nobby Clark (vocals), Dave Paton (guitar) and Billy Lyall (keyboards). Despite Bell's offer,

Gentrys. Produced by Jonathan King, the record made no impression initially, but radio finally picked up on it, and extensive airplay helped it reach Number 9. During the next 18 months, three follow-up singles – 'We Can Make Music', 'Manana' and 'Saturday Night' – flopped, and the group were soon all back doing odd jobs in Edinburgh to make ends meet. Changing their producer to Ken Howard and Alan

group to addresses lifted from the personal columns of pop magazines. And the week 'Remember (Sha-La-La)' was bubbling under, 'Top Of The Pops' viewers saw the famous Rollers outfits for the first time after Eric Faulkner suggested they exaggerate the fashion for rather short trousers that seemed so popular with kids in Scotland.

After four years on the road, however,

Opposite: Woody braces himself for success. Behind him, from left: Les, Derek, Alan and Eric. Above: Fans clamoured to reach their idols whenever the tartan tearaways performed their hits.

however, Paton and Lyall now left the group (later re-surfacing as members of Pilot) and guitarist Neil Henderson and keyboard player Archie Marr were brought in. Subsequently a second guitar player, Eric Faulkner (born 21 October 1954) was added to the line-up and Marr was dropped.

In June 1971, the Rollers' first single was released. Entitled 'Keep On Dancing', it had been a US hit in 1965 for the

Blakley for 'Manana' and then Bill Martin and Phil Coulter for 'Saturday Night' had seemingly little effect on sales, although the fact that 'Saturday Night' became a Number 1 in the US in 1975 and 'Manana' sold well in Europe after winning Luxembourg's International Song Competition suggests that Bell's British promotion machine was not up to scratch.

Milk and alcohol
In February 1974, however, the group's final chance with Bell, another Martin/ Coulter production entitled 'Remember (Sha-La-La)', reached Number 6. Almost in desperation, Paton had publicised the record by sending 10,000 photos of the

the Bay City Rollers were on the verge of splitting up – some members were barely on speaking terms – and only success held the nucleus together. Even a chart record couldn't persuade new guitarist John Devine or Nobby Clark to stay; they quit, grumbling about the tyrannical way Paton prowled around hotel corridors in an attempt to keep the group away from girls. Consequently by the time the next single, 'Shang-A-Lang', spread the first ripples of Rollermania by zipping up the charts to Number 2, the famous line-up of the Longmuir brothers, Eric Faulkner, rhythm guitarist Stuart 'Woody' Wood (born 25 February 1957) and singer Les McKeown (born 12 November 1955), was complete.

At last, the Rollers took off. 'Summer-love Sensation' reached Number 3 in August and 'All Of Me Loves All Of You' made Number 4 two months later, while their first album, *Rollin'*, climbed to the top of the LP charts. Early in 1975, their first session with Phil Wainman, who was to become their regular producer, resulted in their first Number 1 single, 'Bye Bye Baby', and this was followed to the top in July by 'Give A Little Love'. Meanwhile, the ratings of TV pop shows had rocketed with frequent appearances from the Bay City Rollers. They were virtually the resi-

Live from Scotland: The Bay City Rollers hosted their own TV show, 'Shang-A-Lang' (above left and right). Below: The boys toast their manager Tam Paton and his bride-to-be Marcella Knaislova on the occasion of their engagement.

dent group on Mike Mansfield's 'Supersonic' and they were even given their own show, entitled 'Shang-A-Lang'. And no live performance was complete without a stage surrounded by steel barriers and a row of security men, absolutely bewildered by the scenes of adolescent frenzy.

The group's publicity machine unceasingly pushed out an image of the Rollers as non-drinking, non-smoking, hard-working teenagers with no time for girlfriends. 'We never go to parties. If you're at parties all night, it affects your work in the end,' said Paton. And: 'When we travel, we stop and have a milk or something but never ever go into pubs.' But behind the virginal facade, a riot was going on: sexual adventures in hotel bedrooms with teenage fans, experiments with drugs and drunken orgies.

Two of the Rollers, Eric Faulkner and Alan Longmuir, attempted suicide, while

Les McKeown killed an ageing pedestrian in a road accident and was accused of firing an air gun at young fans camped outside his house. Founder member Alan Longmuir eventually left in April 1976, unable to take the pressure any longer (though he rejoined two years later). He was replaced by 17-year-old Ian Mitchell, who was himself replaced after 6 months by Pat McGlynn. It didn't seem to matter who was in the Rollers – it was the collective image that counted.

Image is all

Responsibility for this image – and the group's success and subsequent collapse – can be laid at Tam Paton's door. In the mid Sixties, he had been given a tip by Brian Epstein which, in a fairly unsubtle way, he used to guide the Rollers' entire career. Paton was playing piano in a group called the Crusaders, which broke up after coming tenth in a London talent competition judged by the Beatles' manager. When he approached Epstein afterwards, Paton was told that his group had scored so badly because they lacked a clearly drawn image.

Consequently, when he took on the Rollers, Paton worked through countless ways of presenting his boys – see-through trousers, for instance – before coming up with the one that worked. But he overdid it. So many publicity stories went out about the group not having girlfriends – in order that young record-buyers everywhere could enjoy untrammelled dreams of being the one girl in the world who could make her favourite Roller's life complete – that the press simply assumed the boys were gay. And even though Paton's style may have given the group a brief, frenzied fling at the top, it restricted the wider appeal and musical development they eventually came to want.

In addition, there was nothing of substance *behind* the image. An attempt to give the group complementary personalities like the Beatles – Derek was the quiet one, Woody the prankster – failed because the Rollers were neither bright nor witty enough to stand individual scrutiny. When, for instance, Les was asked why he was in the music business, all he could muster was the stock showbiz reply: 'I guess I get a buzz from making people happy.'

Where previous teenybop idols like the Monkees or Marc Bolan had provoked mild contempt or amusement, the Bay City Rollers inspired an enmity rarely seen in pop music. The *New Musical Express* labelled them 'assembly line androids in clowns' outfits' and even Tam Paton was moved to remark how boring they were: 'We've really got nothing in common. How can you talk to them about politics? I don't think any of them even know who the Prime Minister is.'

Right: La vie en rose – Les McKeown accepts the gift of a flower from an ecstatic young fan.

But their ignorance and vacuity did not prevent an American breakthrough, and in October 1975 they set off on their first US trip. Their nationality was used to package them in much the same way as British groups of the early Sixties. On the Howard Cossell TV show, for instance, Scottish bagpipes set the scene as a huge tartan box, labelled 'Live From Scotland', collapsed to reveal the Rollers playing 'Saturday Night'. The song went on to become a US Number 1 and the group enjoyed America enough to return often.

Back in Britain, however, they managed only two Top Ten hits in 1976 – 'Love Me Like I Love You' and 'I Only Wanna Be With You' – despite a sellout concert tour. When they quit their homeland for tax purposes and embarked on lucrative tours of Japan and the States in the following year, their popularity waned dramatically. British fans were tiring of their bouncy but by now monotonous sound and felt deserted, too.

Back to zero

As their success began to wane, the group members started to quarrel and in August 1978 they sacked Les McKeown (though he said he resigned), claiming that the singer had 'gone all Hollywood' on them, chasing Britt Ekland around Los Angeles when he should have been rehearsing their next album. The egocentric McKeown, incidentally, was so generally unpopular by this stage that when the group were film-ing a 13-part series for the NBC US TV network, a cameraman thrust a custard pie in his face on behalf of the entire production crew, which was fed up with his tantrums.

McKeown was replaced by South African Duncan Faure, but the group, by now, was finished. It was over a year since they had had a UK hit single and finally, in August 1979, Tam Paton received a phonecall dismissing him as manager. 'I took those boys to the top,' he said at the time. 'When they stopped taking my advice, they went on the slide.' He was probably right – even if the image he had given them did contain the seeds of its own destruction.

Two years later, while McKeown was appearing second on the bill to the Nolans in Japan, the Rollers attempted a comeback with the album *Ricochet* on the Epic label. Despite some polite press coverage, no-one was really very interested.

In retrospect, the Bay City Rollers are little more than a name in rock history. They probably retain a place in the affections of the teenyboppers they whipped to such adolescent hysteria. But their contribution to music was absolutely zero.

COLIN SHEARMAN

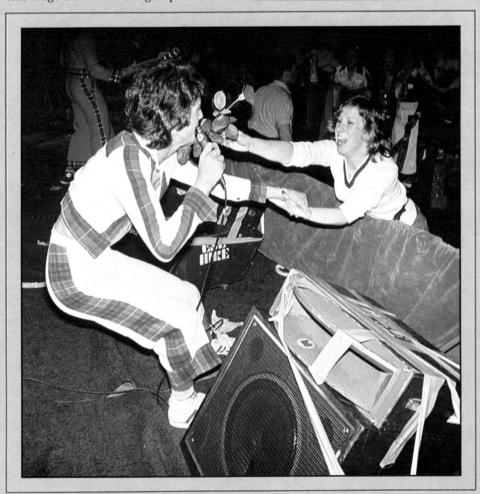

STARDUST MEMORIES

Success struck three times for Shane Fenton

**Alvin Stardust
Recommended Listening**

Greatest Hits (Magnet MAG 4002) (Includes: My Coo-Ca-Choo, Jealous Mind, Red Dress).

Sixties pop star Shane Fenton (above) dons leather to become Alvin Stardust (opposite) Below: Rockabilly Alvin in the Eighties.

THE CAREER OF Alvin Stardust began in the pre-British beat days of the early Sixties. Back then he was known as Shane Fenton and, with backing group the Fentones, enjoyed mild success before the arrival of the Beatles abruptly curtailed their run of chart appearances. But while many of his contemporaries floundered and sank in the post-Beatles boom, never to be heard of again, Fenton was able to engineer a startling comeback a decade later. Following hot on the heels of teen-pop successes T.Rex, Sweet and Gary Glitter, Shane Fenton became Alvin Stardust, a slinky figure in tight black leather and – although rapidly approaching 30 – a teen idol once more.

Cool and moody

Stardust was born Bernard Jewry in the North London suburb of Muswell Hill in September 1944. His family moved to Mansfield, Nottinghamshire, when Bernard was two. Bitten by the rock'n'roll bug in the mid Fifties, Jewry formed a friendship with a local group, Johnny Theakston and the Tremeloes. The group subsequently changed their name to the Fentones and landed a spot on BBC radio's prestigious 'Saturday Club' pop show. Only a few days before their appearance, however, the Fentones singer collapsed and died within 48 hours. Bernard Jewry had occasionally sung with the group at their Palais appearances and was asked to stand in as their vocalist. So Bernard Jewry changed his name to Shane Fenton and fronted the group for the show.

A recording contract eventually followed, and Shane Fenton and the Fentones entered the charts in October 1961 with 'I'm A Moody Guy', which peaked at Number 22. 1962 brought three further Top Forty hits for the group, 'Walk Away', 'It's All Over Now' and 'Cindy's Birthday', the last of which reached Number 19 in August and was the Fentones' biggest hit.

With the Beatles offering something immediately fresh and exciting to British pop, the Fentones' sound became dated virtually overnight. While the Fentones themselves scored a couple of minor instrumental hits – with 'The Mexican' and 'The Breeze And I' in 1962 – Shane Fenton and his group looked set for the obscurity which beckoned so many British rock'n'rollers following the Liverpool boom.

True to form, Fenton and the Fentones made a desultory stab at films, appearing with Billy Fury, Bobby Vee and Helen Shapiro in Michael Winner's 1962 film *Play It Cool*, in which they performed one number, 'It's Gonna Take Magic'. But by 1963 the Beatles and their beat contemporaries had taken control of the charts.

Tired of the constant package tours and their lack of success, the group called it a day, and soon after their dissolution Fenton moved into management; his charges included Lulu and the Hollies, which reunited him with former Fentones' drummer Bobby Elliott. It was to be a long sabbatical from the charts for Fenton, however – and, apart from 'Moody Guy' being revived on the radio, he was all but forgotten.

Following a chance meeting with Michael Levy in the early Seventies, he signed to Levy's recently-founded independent label, Magnet. But it took an astute young writer/producer called Peter Shelley to bring Shane Fenton back from the grave. Shelley was looking for a way to capitalise on the British glam pop boom: if Mike Leander could play Doctor Frankenstein and create a success like Gary Glitter, reasoned Shelley, why couldn't he?

Shelley was an able composer of lightweight pop material – he was to register hits under his own name with 'Gee Baby' in 1974, and the canine nausea of 'Love Me, Love My Dog' in 1975. What Shelley wanted in 1973, though, was someone who could project the image to match a name he had already created – Alvin Stardust.

The leather boy

Bernard Jewry/Shane Fenton was delighted at the opportunity to have another crack at the charts, and recognised the commercial possibilities of Shelley's song, 'My Coo-Ca-Choo'. Within weeks of its release in the autumn of 1973, it had reached Number 2 in the British charts, being kept from the top slot only by teenypop idol David Cassidy's mawkish 'Darlin''/'The Puppy Song', and the single was a Top Ten hit all across Europe and the Far East that same year. 'My Coo-Ca-Choo' was a hypnotically catchy debut for Alvin Stardust and its resonant bass sound and slightly suggestive lyrics were matched by Stardust's glistening stage persona. Clad from neck to toe in black leather, enormous rings glittering on his gloves, coiling the microphone in a manner not seen since Dave Berry's heyday, Alvin Stardust was able to project a kind of virile sensuality which appealed to a pop world up to its eyes in mascara.

In February 1974, the follow-up single, 'Jealous Mind', went one better and made the top of the UK charts. Alvin hit the Top Twenty three more times that year, with 'Red Dress', 'You You You' and 'Tell Me Why'. Shelley's songs were simple pop fare and scarcely original, yet they were enhanced by Stardust's resonant vocals and his love of classic rock'n'roll. Together, Stardust and Shelley filched the best elements of Johnny Kidd and the Pirates and the stage image of Gene Vincent, while hints of Elvis Presley's vocal phrasing could be detected in Stardust's singing.

Then, as quickly as they had arrived, the hits dried up. 'Good Love Can Never Die' reached Number 11 in February 1975, but 'Sweet Cheatin' Rita' could only make it to Number 37. And after that – nothing. Alvin Stardust looked as though he was set to become as much of an anachronism in the Seventies as Shane Fenton had been in the Sixties. Stardust kept plugging away, though, with singles that included a credible and appealing Jonathan King production of Bruce Springsteen's 'Growin' Up'. But this was 1977 and a new age of leather had arrived – the contemporary appeal of punk meant that Alvin Stardust was almost a forgotten man once again.

A Stiff no more

While a new generation charged at the charts, however, there was a renewed fascination in original rock 'n'roll and British pop TV Svengali Jack Good endeavoured to cater for this interest by recreating the fervour of his TV shows of the Fifties. Thus, in the late Seventies, the revived 'Oh Boy' and 'Let It Rock' saw Alvin Stardust sharing the bill with a young singer who was destined to become a star of the Eighties – Shakin' Stevens.

These TV appearances did little to revive Stardust's flagging career – but, just when it seemed as though he would never again grace 'Top Of The Pops', the record company mavericks of Stiff Records stepped in. During their heyday, Stiff (one of whose more memorable mottoes was 'If they're dead – we'll sign 'em!') boasted an awesome new-wave roster, with the Damned, Ian Dury, Elvis Costello, Nick Lowe and Wreckless Eric. But by the early Eighties, apart from Madness, their chart fortunes relied mainly on one-off deals.

Alvin Stardust signed to Stiff in August 1981, and within two months found himself at Number 4 with 'Pretend', a joyous slice of rockabilly performed Eighties-style. It was sufficient to ensure him a slot on that year's Royal Command Performance, where he appeared in a celebration of '25 Years Of British Rock'n'Roll', along with ageing rockers Marty Wilde and Lonnie Donegan – neither of whom had had a sniff of chart success for 20 years.

Stardust's follow-up, 'A Wonderful Time Up There', was a thunderous slab of gospel pop; it failed to reach the heights of 'Pretend' but kept his name in view.

In 1984 he enjoyed his best run of hits since the leather days with 'I Feel Like Buddy Holly' (Number 7), 'I Won't Run Away' (Number 7) and 'So Near To Christmas' (Number 29). Revelling in a new role as born-again Christian, he hosted the TV *Rock Gospel* show and toured with *Godspell*—an evangelist now rather than a rock revivalist, but above all a survivor.

PATRICK HUMPHRIES

Darling David

Above: America's top rock group? The Partridge Family pose on the lawn. Below: David Cassidy shimmers in the spotlight. Opposite: Strumming away at the heartstrings of his youthful following.

David Cassidy
Recommended Listening

Cassidy Live (Bell 243 2308) (Includes: Breaking Up Is Hard To Do, I Am A Clown, How Can I Be Sure, It's Praying On My Mind, Daydreamer, Some Kind Of Summer, Please Please Me).

David Cassidy: teen dream from the TV screen

'CAN AMERICA'S TOP rock group prevail against the evil machinations of a fat but deadly enemy agent – without blowing their cool?' ran the blurb on the back cover of a 1970 US novelette. The writer went on to describe 'America's top rock group' thus: 'They're a high-voltage six-pack of talent and energy – five groovy kids plus one beautiful, mini-skirted Mom – an all-American super-singing weapon.' And just who *were* 'America's top rock group'? The book's title provided the answer: *The Partridge Family*.

In November 1970, the Partridge Family's 'I Think I Love You' reached the top of the US charts while 'I'll Meet You Halfway' and 'Doesn't Somebody Want To Be Wanted' both made the Top Ten the following year. But it was not through recording rock songs in the family garage that the Partridge Family had made it to the top; it was through being six TV actors contracted to a series about a clean young American family whose hobby was making music together. The kids had the usual problems – what to wear to high-school dances, unsightly braces on their teeth, disastrous blind dates and unrequited crushes. The fact that they had to go out on the road and play in the family pop group was almost incidental to the show's plots or the programme's appeal. 'The Partridge Family' had more in common with 'The Brady Bunch' or 'My Three Sons' than it did with 'The Monkees' (where music *had* played an essential part in proceedings); nevertheless, spin-off records credited to the Partridge Family (and played by Hollywood session musicians) made the charts. And they made a pop star out of David Cassidy, the actor who portrayed Keith and, apart from the occasional contribution by Shirley Jones, was the only cast member who actually sang on any of the recordings.

Shirley's boy
David Cassidy was born in New York on 12 April 1950, the son of actor Jack Cassidy. After leaving college, David took up acting himself, working for the Los Angeles Theatre Group. By 1968, he was landing regular TV work in such series as 'Ironside', 'The Survivors', 'Marcus Welby MD', 'Bonanza' and 'The Mod Squad'. Then in early 1970, his stepmother Shirley Jones was contracted by Screen Gems-Columbia (who had been behind the Monkees show) to star in a new pop-oriented soap opera entitled 'The Partridge Family'. Jones – a screen actress/singer of some repute who had starred in *Oklahoma!* (1955), *Carousel* (1956) and *The Music Man* (1962) and won an Oscar for her performance in *Elmer Gantry* (1960) – suggested that her stepson play her son Keith in the TV show. Cassidy's pretty, fresh-faced looks were in keeping with the traditional US teen idol image; also, he was a competent singer.

'The Partridge Family' was an immediate hit, although the music that accompanied it was dull and staid even by teenybop standards. Producer Wes Farrell wrote or co-wrote many of the songs himself, making up the numbers by dredging up old hits like Neil Sedaka's 'Breaking Up Is Hard To Do' and Gene Pitney's 'Looking Through The Eyes Of Love' and re-arranging them with more than a degree of mediocrity. But Cassidy's baby face and breathy vocals sold the product, and it was inevitable that he would soon be recording in his own right.

Confessions of a pop idol
In 1971, 'Cherish', a solo reworking of the Association's 1966 hit, reached Number 9 in the US charts, while the first album released under his name, also called *Cherish*, sold a million. The LP's music was bland, sanitised, middle-of-the-road pop – but with the force of TV and teen magazines behind him, Cassidy's success seemed unstoppable. But then, in March 1972, the actor/singer was guilty of a disastrous error when, in a *Rolling Stone* interview, he made some 'startling' confessions. He loathed his role in 'The Partridge Family', he said. He had dabbled with drugs and he quite liked sex! The Keith Partridge boy-next-door myth was exploded and his popularity in the States began to dwindle.

Cassidy's three 1972 singles, 'Could It Be Forever', 'How Can I Be Sure' and 'Rock Me Baby' all failed to reach the Top Twenty so, in mid 1973, Cassidy and management turned their attentions to Britain, where a teen-pop revival was in full swing. Furthermore, 'The Partridge Family' was being networked on English television – a fact that had helped 'I Think I Love You' and 'It's One Of Those Nights (Yes Love)' into the UK Top Twenty and

'Breaking Up Is Hard To Do' and 'Looking Through The Eyes Of Love' into the Top Ten. In April 1972, Cassidy's solo 'Could It Be Forever' had reached Number 2, while 'How Can I Be Sure' had given him a chart-topper six months later.

Leaving home
In October 1973, Cassidy arrived in London to try to capitalise on his fame. A couple of interviews and a mime to his new record 'Daydreamer' on 'Top Of The Pops' was enough to send the single to the top. Yet, although this seemed to augur well for the future, Cassidy was by now tiring of his teen-idol role. At the end of 1973, he left 'The Partridge Family' – the series ended as a result – and, after a hysterical London concert in the spring of 1974 during which a fan was crushed to death, he decided to reshape his career and attempt to appeal to a more mature rock audience.

Signing to RCA, Cassidy enlisted the help of such reputable figures as ex-Beach Boy Bruce Johnston, Poco's Richie Furay, Mark Volman and Howard Kaylan (alias Flo and Eddie) and Harry Nilsson to produce the aptly-titled album *The Higher They Climb The Harder They Fall* (1975). But this, and his subsequent albums *Home Is Where The Heart Is* (1976) and *Gettin' It In The Street* (1977), revealed only an average talent and a dearth of ideas.

Cassidy had been a victim – initially a willing one – of an American entertainment industry that had long since realised that almost anything could sell provided the packaging and image was right and sufficiently exposed. The music had been secondary to swoony looks and hints of sex. Cassidy made a surprise comeback to the UK charts in early 1985, having signed to Arista, with the Number 6 single 'Last Kiss'. A run as lead in Dave Clark's musical *Time* followed.   TOM HIBBERT

1517

The Odd Couple

How the Mael brothers made Sparks fly

'THERE ARE SOME TERRIFIC records get out and that people just will not buy because of the image . . . for instance, Sparks. They were always one of my favourite groups: they had a man with a silly haircut, and that was great for one record – see the man who looks like Hitler. But three records on they're making really, really great singles and things, and lyrics that said a lot about what was going on, but no-one wanted to go into a record shop and buy something by a man who looked like Hitler. It was stupid.'

The comments of the Human League's Phil Oakey in 1983 highlighted the reason for the ultimate commercial failure of one of the most original pop groups of the Seventies. Significantly, Oakey himself had discarded his own 'silly haircut' shortly after the Human League broke through to a mass audience. But for all their awareness of the foibles, frailties and self-consciousness of others, Ron and Russell Mael of Sparks always seemed careless of the image they themselves were creating. They never realised when the joke – that of the beady-eyed weirdo with the slicked-back hair and toothbrush moustache giving piano accompaniment to the *castrato* pretty-boy singer – had worn painfully thin.

In 1981, seven years after they first stunned audiences with that bizarre juxtaposition of spooky inscrutability and winsome sex appeal, they still appeared the same. Visually, Sparks didn't have a clue how to develop beyond mere novelty value. Despite that, or maybe in keeping with it, they were masters of ephemeral pop, perfecting the trash aesthetic in a handful of tinselly singles and on at least one album.

Amateur hour
The Mael brothers were born in Los Angeles – Ron in 1949, Russell in 1951 – and were guided into showbiz at an early age by parents who put them on the stage. They went on to study film, graphics and English at UCLA and there in 1968 formed their first band, Halfnelson, with Ron on piano and organ, Russell singing and Earle Mankey playing guitar. The next two years were spent putting together demo tapes (many of the songs inspired by movies) until one attracted the Philadelphia singer-guitarist Todd Rundgren, who was then making his mark as a producer on the Bearsville label.

Signing them up, Rundgren produced the group's first LP in Hollywood with Earle's younger brother Jim coming in on bass and guitar and Harley Feinstein on drums. Released in January 1972, *Halfnelson* flopped miserably. The band changed its name to Sparks and re-released the LP under that title, but with the same result.

A European tour that ignited little interest was followed by a second album, *A*

Woofer In Tweeter's Clothing (1972), on which the Maels began to find some creative form. The LP didn't sell well, but it did establish the quirkiness and continental preoccupations that would become Sparks trademarks. 'The Louvre', sung in French, 'Girl From Germany' (issued as a single years later in the UK) and a delicious soft-rock version of 'Do Re Mi' showcased Russell's voice, at this stage a silky, stylised lisp, which – a few octaves higher and more frenetic – would soon give Sparks their definitive sound.

Their eccentricity was always more likely to catch the imagination of British rather than the more staid American audiences, as the Maels discovered when they moved to Britain in 1973, quickly getting a recording contract with Island. In May 1974 they appeared on BBC-TV's 'Top Of The Pops', and no-one knew what to make of them at all. Russell's appeal was obvious and he subsequently became a teen pin-up mobbed by girls at concerts, but his uncoordinated dancing, allied to Ron's chilling sidelong glances over the top of his piano at the TV cameras, were very odd – enough to propel the peerless neurotic grandeur of 'This Town Ain't Big Enough For The Both Of Us' to Number 2 in the charts.

Sparks' finest three minutes, the song – a careering homage to pre-date anxiety – was ushered in by Ron's twitchily chiming piano, hit a sensational stomping beat with ricocheting gunfire and Russell's querulous falsetto, and was finally cut to pieces by Trevor White's scything guitar. For the rest of 1974, Sparks were a very big name, re-entering the Top Ten with 'Amateur Hour', another Sparks comment about adolescent sex, which climbed to Number 7.

Punning pop
Both hits were taken from *Kimono My House*, a consummate pop album produced by Muff Winwood, with White, drummer Dinky Diamond and bassist Ian Hampton completing the new Sparks line-up. It was an ambitious affair bursting with finely crafted, highly literate and acerbic Ron Mael songs, the best of which, apart from the singles, were the shrill and insistent 'Equator', and 'Thank God It's Not Christmas' with its hypnotic ebb and flow, crashing chords and wry, ennui-inspired lyrics. *Kimono My House* reached Number 4 in the UK album charts in June, and it was as clever, thrilling and seductive as anything from that inventive late glam-rock era.

Sparks toured Britain in the autumn of 1974, proving nothing – for they were never a successful live band, restricted on stage by the apparent narrowness of their appeal – and released a new album, *Propaganda*, which repeated the *Kimono My House* formula and offered no fresh surprises. The band's chart places immediately began to slip: the LP reached Number 9; its single cuts, the comparatively subdued 'Never Turn Your Back On

Opposite: Sparks fly around the Mael brothers – Ron (left) and Russell. Above: Sparks in the Kimono My House *era. Below: In France in the late Seventies.*

Mother Earth' and 'Something For The Girl With Everything', peaked in turn at Numbers 13 and 17.

The *Indiscreet* album of 1975 saw Sparks gently entering a transitional phase. The keyboards/falsetto blend still dominated, but Ron's writing and the arrangements showed signs of greater eclecticism. It was still an oddball collection: the marching beat and thunderous bass of 'Hospitality On Parade' standing alongside 'It Ain't 1918', a *Biergarten* hop with Russell sounding like Marlene Dietrich. The

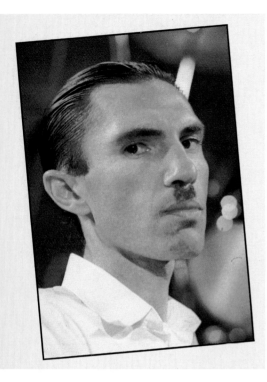

drenched Sparks in a disco tide. Ron's synthesisers now came to the fore and the phased, sophisticated Europop fizz of 'The Number One Song In Heaven' and 'Beat The Clock' lifted Sparks to Numbers 14 and 10 in the British singles charts; both surfaced on the *No 1 In Heaven* LP, which was more Moroder than the Maels.

Following a further collaboration with the producer on *Terminal Jive* (1980), the Maels returned to the old, familiar Sparks sound with the 1981 LP *Whomp That Sucker*, released on Why-Fi Records with US band Bates Motel providing backing. This contained more advice for young lovers in 'Tips For Teens' and saw the return of Russell's highly-strung vocals, for example on 'That's Not Nastassia' – seemingly a nod at film-star Kinski. This was the witty, wonderful Sparks of the mid Seventies, the image intact and eternally silly. In 1982 the Maels recorded an album, *Angst In My Pants*, on Columbia for US release, and recruited four new Sparks for live work. At last their satirical songs had begun to make an impact in the USA.

Sparks continued to fly, always likely to

Above left: Ron Mael's chilling Hitler glance. Above right: Russell at the microphone. Below: Sparks in the Eighties.

singles taken from it, the classy Swing-era 'Looks, Looks, Looks' and the jolly 'Get In The Swing', barely scraped into the Top Thirty, however, while a sixth album, *Big Beat* (1976), sank without trace.

The Maels stressed their support for punk in 1977 but, unable to compete with it themselves, returned to America before moving to Germany and signing to Virgin Records. In 1979, they re-emerged with a reshaped sound courtesy of Donna Summer's producer Giorgio Moroder, who

come up with a cheeky chart entry. Their influence may not have been widespread but their hits, especially 'This Town Ain't Big Enough For The Both Of Us', remained as immediate and exciting as when first released. The 1982-83 boom in electro-pop 'odd couples' – such as Soft Cell, Blancmange, Yazoo and Tears for Fears – saw a return to a format Sparks once seemed to have copyrighted, although the Hitler moustache remained Ron Mael's alone. GRAHAM FULLER

All That Jazz

Rock energy and jazz sophistication made for a brief, exciting union

WHATEVER JAZZ-ROCK IS, it is not just jazz musicians playing solos over rock rhythms. It is a specific style that grew up over a number of years from a number of sources, and that had sufficient musical unity both to be recognised as a style in its own right and eventually to choose its own musical direction. The problem is that it is essentially a fusion of two musics whose basic aim is usually totally different. Jazz and rock have contrasting ideologies, although the musical building blocks they use may be very similar, or in many cases identical. Jazz is very much a music of personal expression, in which the individual pushes himself to ever more intense degrees of communication, often measuring himself against the technical problems of his instrument or the difficulties of the musical form he has chosen. Rock, on the other hand, is about the promulgation of a more general – more social – expression in which the subtleties or introspection of jazz may be completely out of place.

In spite of these aesthetic differences, there are factors that inevitably draw rock and jazz together. The first, and most important, is that both are part of the American popular music tradition. A 12-bar blues in B flat uses the same basic chords whether played in the style of blues singer Robert Johnson, the Glenn Miller Orchestra, John Coltrane or the New York Dolls. These different ways of playing interrelate at many levels; a certain basic facility enables a musician to join different types of groups and to play in any number of different styles before he becomes established in any one of them.

Another major similarity between American jazz and rock, apart from the common elements in their musical tradition, is that both operate under certain important commercial restraints – basically, the need to appeal to a paying audience, whether of record buyers or club and concert-goers.

Between 1965 and 1975 a variety of these common factors drew jazz and rock together. While some critics might argue that the results of this fusion were disappointing, certain musicians managed to amalgamate jazz techniques with the power and general appeal of rock, creating work of lasting worth.

Through the sound barrier

Jazz, of course, was one of the traditions from which rock'n'roll and rockabilly had emerged in the mid Fifties. During the early years of rock, however, the two musics had little time for each other.

Jazz musicians despised rock as simple, vulgar, containing no opportunities for personal expression and designed solely to extract the maximum amount of money from the pockets of gullible young people. Rock musicians, meanwhile, found jazz arid, wrapped up in dry technicalities and saying little they could relate to.

During the early to mid Sixties, a new generation of jazz musicians began to come of age. These were people to whom rock was not some alien monster that had suddenly arisen; rather, it was part of their musical heritage, a sound that, like the blues or R&B, had been a part of the musical wallpaper as they were growing up. Unlike their Fifties predecessors, these younger musicians were not worried by the harmonic simplicity of rock; the avant-garde jazz of the early Sixties represented by Ornette Coleman or John Coltrane was turning its back on the harmonic complexities of previous jazz. At the same time, rock had developed a sufficiently large body of tunes for jazzmen to utilise them – rather as they had mined the rich musical vein of popular stage and film musicals in the Thirties and Forties.

Early attempts at a fusion of jazz and rock elements were hardly convincing, however. When jazzmen tried to investigate the country tradition, as in Jimmy Giuffre's *The Train And The River* (1958), Bob Brookemeyer's tune 'Jive-Hoot' or Gary Burton's *Country Roads And Other Places* (1968), the results were sometimes charming, but hardly powerful; and when black pop was investigated, as in pianist Ramsey Lewis' versions of Stevie Wonder's 'Uptight (Everything's Alright)' and Dobie Gray's 'The "In" Crowd', the records could

Miles Davis blows his own trumpet. The veteran horn player's move to electric instrumentation, initially motivated by competition from the rock field, sent shock waves through the jazz establishment and almost single-handedly ushered in the jazz-rock era.

hardly be said to have shaken the world with their intensity.

But these were merely examples of a growing trend for jazz musicians to look to rock for sources of inspiration. Musicians all over the world could see that there must be a way of combining the two styles; and tunes such as Herbie Hancock's funky (in the early Sixties meaning of the word) 'Watermelon Man' were more successful examples of stylistic fusion. In the UK, too, artists such as Brian Auger and Graham Bond were working towards combining the two; while in the US, groups were formed with the express intention of putting jazz into rock or vice versa. This was sometimes commercially a very happy union – as when Blood, Sweat and Tears and Chicago played rock with a horn section – but a coherent style proved hard to develop.

To the limit and beyond

What was needed was a way of playing in which personal expression could be combined with the widespread popularity of rock. The breakthrough came via the rapid developments in progressive rock from 1966 to 1970 and the experiments of Miles Davis. The jazz musicians who had been putting rock into their music in the mid Sixties had been using rock elements, but had not necessarily seen them as having any great expressive potential in themselves; then, in 1966 and 1967, Jimi Hendrix and Cream showed that rock had the potential within itself to be as intense as any other style. Hendrix in particular extended the possibilities of his instrument as much as any jazzman had done in the past.

The sudden expansion of progressive rock had a particularly important influence on the leading jazz trumpeter Miles Davis. Although the motivations of this complex, prickly personality are hard to fathom, there seems little doubt that falling record sales in the mid Sixties contributed to his desire to investigate the electric instruments that his more commercially successful rock rivals were using. Members of his late Sixties groups such as saxplayer Wayne Shorter, pianists Herbie Hancock and Chick Corea and drummer Tony Williams (who in 1969 formed a real 'fusion' group, Lifetime, using Jack Bruce of Cream on bass, organist Larry Young and guitarist John McLaughlin) were also very interested in new possibilities.

Miles' early experiments (the 1968 LP *Filles De Kilimanjaro*, for example) were not very exciting – especially in comparison with the greatness of his previous work. But in 1969 he released *In A Silent Way*, a record that in its magical, relaxed mood showed precisely how jazz could meet rock. The following year came *Bitches Brew*, the title of which mirrored the swirl of elements in the music. Miles had shown how it could be done – and, while he continued in similar vein (albeit meeting with diminishing critical acclaim) until late in the Seventies when ill-health forced him into temporary retirement, other musicians took what he had done and used it as the basis for their own work. Donald Byrd, former hard-bop trumpeter, developed a simpler, more overtly funky style that brought him great financial success on the West Coast in the early Seventies; the Jazz

Crusaders, who had played Sixties-style funk, dropped the word 'jazz' from their name, and began playing and composing in a laid-back, sophisticated style, thereby achieving massive popularity.

The boiling point

Perhaps the most important of the groups formed in the early Seventies was, however, the Mahavishnu Orchestra. Under John McLaughlin's inspired leadership, this group put together *The Inner Mounting Flame* in 1971. With its sudden time changes, its breathtaking guitar solos and the precise but powerful drumming of Billy Cobham, this LP marked one of the creative high-points of jazz-rock.

The pianists who had played on Miles Davis' *In A Silent Way* all went on to form outstandingly successful groups. Chick Corea's Return to Forever, for some time featuring the great bass-player Stanley Clarke, tended towards the Latin side of jazz-rock. Joe Zawinul formed Weather Report with Wayne Shorter and although the group had problems finding the ideal rhythm section, it remained consistently popular; in addition Herbie Hancock also found fame and fortune with a solo career, including a Seventies funk remake of 'Watermelon Man'.

The Inner Mounting Flame had proved to be the peak of jazz-rock, however. The jazz-rock groups enjoyed – and many have maintained – great popularity, but some time in the mid Seventies their ability to add anything creative to rock seemed to die. Groups like those of trumpet and flugelhorn player Chuck Mangione and sax player Grover Washington Jr continued to produce records that sold millions, while great jazz musicians who cared to turn their hand to playing music with a funky beat – trumpeter Freddie Hubbard for example – found the royalties flowing in. But something was missing.

Jazz-rock had gained a certain vitality from its connection with rock, but it gradually became the sound of filler music on TV shows, or in advertisements where a certain hip but not too young image was required. Jazz-rock built up its own establishment, its own set of musicians who tended to play in each other's bands and who considered themselves jazz musicians. These people saw themselves using rock styles merely as an aid to mass communication or mass money-making, depending upon which way you looked at it. In 1978, John McLaughlin, who had moved in new directions since 1975, was scathing about the path the music he had done so much to mould was taking: 'How do I feel about jazz-rock? Boring! It bores me to tears; it just doesn't go anywhere.'

By the early Eighties, jazz-rock was no longer part of rock; the nearest it got was in its close links with the technically expert but emotionally dead hand of disco-funk, or when its musicians were used as session men (Steve Gadd's excellent drumming on Paul Simon's '50 Ways To Leave Your Lover' for example). By then it was hard to believe how, in the early Seventies, the great combination of tastes and attitudes had put *Bitches Brew* on record shelves along with, say, *Led Zeppelin II*, Joni Mitchell's *Clouds* and Frank Zappa's *Hot Rats*. While rock changes with each generation, however, jazz musicians just seem to get older playing the same kind of music.   ASHLEY BROWN

Chick Corea (above), John McLaughlin (left) and Herbie Hancock (below) were all former members of Miles Davis' band who went on to make names for themselves as jazz-rock performers. Keyboardist Corea's Return to Forever also featured virtuoso bassist Stanley Clarke (second from left).

East met West in the music of John McLaughlin

'MAHAVISHNU' was the name given to John McLaughlin by his guru, Sri Chinmoy, during that period in the Seventies when McLaughlin was a disciple of Chinmoy's philosophy/religion. It is hardly surprising, then, that the mention of the Mahavishnu Orchestra will always evoke first the image of its guitarist-leader, clothed in white, wearing a benign smile but totally committed to and in charge of the music going on around him. Most of the composer credits on the Mahavishnu albums give just one name – his. Interviews in the music papers in the Seventies were invariably with him, although one of the other members of the band would occasionally be asked in awed tones what it was like working with John McLaughlin. When any news or details of the Orchestra's current philosophy was to be sought, every journalist immediately went to the fountainhead.

This is not to suggest, however, that McLaughlin deliberately surrounded himself with docile, subservient musicians

who were only there to play his music, or that he chose sidemen who could only reach a mediocre level of playing and would never compete for the limelight. On the contrary, he has always played with the best in terms of technique, enthusiasm and imagination. If McLaughlin is the man most associated with the Mahavishnu Orchestra, it is because he was its instigator, he was always obviously in charge, and he never ran out of ideas or energy; when the time came to make a change he was not afraid to start again with a completely new line-up.

McLaughlin was born on 4 January 1942 in Yorkshire, England. He started playing guitar in his teens and first gained prominence with British R&B bands such as the Graham Bond Organisation and Brian Auger and the Trinity. His solo album *Extrapolation* (1969) marked his crossover into jazz. He soon became a member of Lifetime and also featured on Miles Davis' *In A Silent Way* (1969) and *Bitches Brew* (1970). By the end of that year, McLaughlin had achieved almost legendary status; the time was clearly ripe for him to form his own group. He began the process after recording *My Goal's Beyond* (1971).

Flaming fusion

The first incarnation of the Orchestra comprised Jan Hammer (born 17 April 1948) on keyboards, Jerry Goodman on violin, Billy Cobham (born 16 May 1944) on drums and Rick Laird on bass. With the possible exception of Laird, they were all players of proven ability from diverse backgrounds, capable of tackling any style of music around (and some that had hitherto not existed) at any tempo this side of the speed of light. Goodman and Cobham had first played with McLaughlin on *My Goal's Beyond*.

The Inner Mounting Flame was recorded in the summer of 1971 and gave notice that McLaughlin was not content merely to consolidate the pollwinner's status he had reached as a result of records with Miles Davis and other major jazz/fusion musicians. Here was a sound that was electric and yet not banal rock, music that was subtle and intelligent without being sterile or elitist.

The inevitable round of gigs followed – clubs, then large theatres and festivals as the band's reputation deservedly grew. The music developed with all the live playing until, when the album *Birds Of Fire* appeared in 1973, the Mahavishnu trademarks of adrenalin-fuelled intensity and impossible tempos mastered without apparent effort were legendary. This album and *Between Nothingness And Eternity*, the album recorded live in New York's Central Park in August of the same year, probably give the best picture of the first Mahavishnu Orchestra at the height of its power – sounding as if the highly orchestrated sections were being played for the first time and improvising with verve and fire, as the studio album's title suggested.

From the very first phased gong smashes leading into similarly treated arpeggios on guitar and keyboards, *Birds Of Fire* evoked an atmosphere, a feeling that a journey was being embarked upon. The guitar and violin sang a wailing theme over the driving rhythm section, the various parts coming together in a complex meter that galloped away, whipped on by Cobham's knife-edge cymbals. Many musicians are snobbish about speeding up, but the title track of *Birds Of Fire* was allowed to leap ahead rather than being held back to a strict machine-like tempo.

For all McLaughlin's famed guitar-technique, he confined his own solos to terse, concise statements, never apparently trying to amaze the listener or his fellow musicians with chorus after chorus of pyrotechnics but spurting out short phrases and bending a few vital notes before taking up the theme again. On the track 'Resolution', the guitar, violin and synthesiser

Left: McLaughlin the mystic is captured in typical pose. Above right: The first incarnation of the Orchestra, with drummer Billy Cobham and keyboardist Jan Hammer. Below: A later line-up.

almost held a conversation, swapping comments and suggestions while the bass and drums kept a steady back beat. It demonstrated what excellent musicians Hammer and Goodman were in their own right, as well as how equal in importance all the members were, Laird's bass providing a steady foundation beneath the others.

East meets West

After three years McLaughlin felt the need for a change. Michael Walden replaced Cobham, bringing a different, supple percussion feeling, ex-Motown sessioneer Ralphe Armstrong took over the bass and Gayle Moran played keyboards. Various others played from time to time around this nucleus, including violinist Jean-Luc Ponty, who had been with Frank Zappa after leaving his native France. The album most representative of the second half of the Orchestra's life was 1974's epic *Apocalypse*, produced by George Martin, which featured tight group playing surrounded by string-orchestra sections scored by Mike Gibbs.

Then, following McLaughlin's break with his guru, the Mahavishnu Orchestra was allowed to die a natural death, having fulfilled its purpose of expressing McLaughlin's musical philosophy in the early and mid Seventies. What followed was the much more intimate Shakti, a band of Indian musicians, acoustic and almost totally Oriental in concept, while the subsequent One Truth Band lay somewhere between East and West. After the demise of that band, McLaughlin returned to his pre-Mahavishnu state, appearing with other superstars of jazz/fusion and issuing occasional (mostly acoustic) solo albums under his own name.

HUGH HOPPER

John McLaughlin and the Mahavishnu Orchestra Recommended Listening

Birds Of Fire (CBS 65321) (Includes: Miles Beyond, Celestial Terrestrial Commuters, Hope, Resolution, Sanctuary); *Inner Mounting Flame* (CBS 64717) (Includes: A Lotus On Irish Streams, Vital Transformation, The Dance Of Maya, Awakening).

Platinum sounds from an unfashionable supergroup

CHICAGO ARE one of the enigmas of rock. A large part of the rock audience has no time for them; critics have been vitriolic about them from the outset. The group maintained broadly the same line-up and remained a self-sufficient unit. Rarely was the assistance of other artists sought and rarely did its members undertake outside assignments. Chicago didn't impinge on the rest of the rock world, and the group remained unaffected by outside developments. They charted their own introspective course – and in doing so sold millions of albums.

The group was formed in Chicago in 1967. There were seven original members: Robert Lamm (keyboards and lead vocals); Pete Cetera (bass and vocals); Terry Kath

(lead guitar and vocals); James Pankow (trombone); Lee Loughnane (trumpet); Walter Parazaider (woodwind) and Dan Seraphine (drums). Pankow, Seraphine, Parazaider and Loughnane all received formal training in music at Chicago's De Paul University. Around the mid Sixties they formed the Big Thing (a name inspired by the city's Mafia connections), together with Lamm, who met the others on the local club circuit. Cetera joined them in 1966, and Kath the following year, just after they had dropped their name at the suggestion of James William Guercio, also a former De Paul student, who was to become their mentor.

Under their new name of Chicago Transit Authority they played seedy bars and small clubs throughout the Midwest, but with little success. Guercio, however, had established his own reputation on the West Coast with his production of Blood, Sweat

and Tears; he invited Chicago Transit Authority to join him out there, where he thought they might fare better.

Guercio found them dates at prestigious venues like the Whiskey-A-Go-Go on Sunset Strip. He also persuaded CBS to sign the group, in spite of the company's reservations that the band sounded too similar to Blood, Sweat and Tears. He also conceived one of rock's most successful marketing campaigns. The group's debut album *Chicago Transit Authority* (1968) was a double, and retailed very cheaply in the record shops.

Their sound was calculated to arouse interest. Blood, Sweat and Tears had proved there was a market for jazz-rock. Chicago Transit Authority, however, were based more firmly in rock; despite their jazz leanings, they had a white soul sound, with a four-piece rhythm section and a brass trio.

Chanting for change

At the time, audiences were searching for something of more cultural weight, and Chicago Transit Authority fitted the bill. The music, with its jazz sequences and long solos, seemed sophisticated without ever being difficult. Lamm's lyrics, though informed by the revolutionary rhetoric of the times, were notable largely for their superficiality. However the group – or Guercio – had the striking idea of starting side four with chants recorded during the demonstrations at the 1968 Democratic Convention in Chicago. This ploy cemented the group's identification with both the city and the counter-culture.

The Chicago Transit Authority duly became the first Columbia act to be accredited with a certified platinum album, even though the label boasted such names as Bob Dylan and Simon and Garfunkel. Lamm's 'Does Anybody Really

Below: Chicago in concert – slick jazz-rock with a three-piece brass section and percussion well to the fore.

Know What Time It Is' and a splendid version of the Spencer Davis Group's 'I'm A Man' (which became a UK Top Ten single) were particularly exciting tracks.

It was in Guercio's pretentious sleeve-notes for that first album that the band's name emerged: 'If you must call them something, speak of the city where all save one were born; where all of them were schooled and bred, and where all of this incredible music went down barely noticed; call them Chicago.' Chicago it was, and that served as the title of the second album, also a double, released in 1970. This repeated the commercial success of its predecessor, and provided major hit singles in 'Make Me Smile' by Pankow, and Lamm's enduringly infectious '25 Or 6 To 4'.

The third album, *Chicago III*, moved into the US Top Ten within weeks of its release early in 1971. This was again a double. The fourth, *Live At Carnegie Hall*, broke the sequence; that was a quadruple. Nevertheless, these demands on the pockets and time of their fans proved anything but counter-productive; by the end of 1971, the group had all four releases in the US album charts.

By that time their appeal had changed completely. Under Guercio's influence, they lost their exciting blend of jazz and rock and their improvisational energy as early as the second album. Their music became increasingly smooth and mechanical, and Lamm's lyrics seemed increasingly effete. Few groups could maintain a consistently high standard at such a rate of production (the equivalent of ten albums in a little under three years), and the four-album live set was particularly weak.

Critics' choice
Nevertheless, Chicago maintained their commercial appeal despite alienating the critics. The group's work attracted increasingly hostile reviews, and by 1973 Lamm was repaying bile with bile through the leadenly obvious 'Critics' Choice' on *Chicago VI*. The band's ranks were swelled by the addition of Brazilian percussionist Laudir deOliveira in 1974 – the year that Lamm released a solo album, *Skinny Boy*. In 1976 the ballad 'If You Leave Me Now' went to Number 1 on both sides of the Atlantic, and became one of the biggest-selling singles of the year.

By now, however, the group were becoming disenchanted with Guercio, whom they considered to be over-scrupulous in his management of the group's affairs, refusing permission for them to appear in the *Sgt Pepper* movie (1978), playing 'Got To

Above, from left: Pete Cetera, Danny Seraphine, Robert Lamm, Lee Loughnane, Terry Kath, Walter Parazaider and James Pankow. Below: Terry Kath in action.

Get You Into My Life'. (Their role was eventually taken by Earth, Wind and Fire, but the film was, ironically, an unmitigated disaster.) At the end of 1977, Chicago and Guercio parted company.

Tragic ending
On 23 January 1978 Terry Kath killed himself while playing with a pistol. For months, the future of the band was in doubt, but they appointed a new manager, Jeff Wald (Helen Reddy's husband) and resumed work. Their next album actually had a title, *Hot Streets*, and a group photograph on the cover. They replaced Kath with ex-Stephen Stills sideman Donnie Dacus, whose playing was noticeably less assertive than that of his predecessor.

Ticket sales for their 1978 tour were slightly disappointing, but fans were reassured by the band's evident enthusiasm.

Co-produced by Phil Ramone, *Hot Streets* provided the band with its twelfth consecutive platinum album. Their 1979 release, *Chicago XIII*, only achieved gold status, however, and for *Chicago XIV*, the band called in veteran producer Tom Dowd. By this time, Dacus, who had never really fitted in, had been replaced by Chris Pinnick, though the absence of Kath's telling guitar contributions, which had offset the increasing blandness, was still felt.

Bill Champlin was added on keyboards in 1982, while Peter Cetera departed in 1985 to score two solo chart-toppers in 'Glory Of Love' and 'The Next Time I Fall'. As vocalist on hit ballads like 'Hard To Say I'm Sorry' (Number 1, 1982), 'Hard Habit To Break' and 'You're The Inspiration' (both Number 3, 1984) Chicago missed him.

BOB WOFFINDEN

MILES AHEAD

Was trumpeter Miles Davis jazz-rock's leading light?

MILES DAVIS' POSITION as a catalyst in music is unique. In the late Forties his short-lived *The Birth Of The Cool* band laid the foundations for what was to develop into the West Coast 'cool' school of jazz playing. Ten years later, he was one of the two major figures (the other being Ornette Coleman) whose experimentation led to the break-up of jazz as it was then known. From being a music where one style was prominent, it became one where many different styles of music co-existed. Within this new-found freedom Davis later initiated an approach using electric instruments and modern recording techniques that had further repercussions in the jazz world and led to jazz-rock and fusion music. Many of the main people involved in this movement first made their name with Davis.

Throughout all these changes Davis' own trumpet-playing remained very much the same. The packaging and the support may have changed but his sense of lyricism, his use of space and his brittle tone, once likened to 'a man walking on egg-shells', were instantly recognisable.

Part of his uniqueness had been established very early, in Alton, Illinois, where Davis was born on 26 May 1926. His first teacher said: 'Play without any vibrato. You're gonna get old anyway and start shaking.' At 19, Miles went to New York, ostensibly to study 'legit' at Juilliard School of Music. He later recalled: 'I spent my first week and my first month's allowance looking for Charlie Parker.' Parker was at that time engaged in changing the nature of jazz by moving from the steady, swinging approach of a band like Count Basie's to the nervous freneticism and complexities of what became known as bop. Although Davis failed to match up to the range and technical abilities of Parker's regular trumpeter Dizzy Gillespie, his recordings and public appearances with Parker were sufficient to mark him out as a young musician to watch.

Further interest was shown, at least by fellow-musicians, when he formed a nine-piece group in 1948 that featured French horn and tuba in addition to the more normal jazz instruments. Along with musicians such as John Lewis, Gerry

Mulligan and Gil Evans, Davis applied some new, almost orchestral, thinking to the musical advances made by bebop; the result was the excellent and highly influential album *The Birth Of The Cool* (1948). Both the ideas and the musicians associated with this record were of great importance in the development of the 'cool' school, a fresh, subtle style of music prominent on the West Coast in the Fifties.

Davis was involved with Gil Evans again in the late Fifties when they recorded three albums extending the approach used in *The Birth Of The Cool* in a magnificent way. These albums, *Miles Ahead* (1957), *Sketches Of Spain* (1959) and *Porgy And Bess* (1959), placed Miles in sumptuously orchestrated surroundings and were highly acclaimed.

They also gave Miles access to a new approach to improvising which was to affect his thinking quite radically: 'Gil only wrote a scale for me to play. No chords. This gives you a lot more freedom and space to hear things.' That approach was not new to jazz but it was Davis who codified it in the stunning 1959 album, *Kind Of Blue*. Davis had spoken of the 'infinite possibilities' of such an approach, and these were demonstrated on this album in various ways. Firstly there were

the different approaches of the separate compositions to this scalic method: 'So What' was based on a 32-bar standard song form, and used one scale only, transposing it for the middle eight; 'Flamenco Sketches' used five scales, with the soloist playing each until he wished to move to the next. Then, within the pieces, Miles approached his solos lyrically, playing mostly notes from the scale, while saxophone player John Coltrane played in a more complex way, using the scale as a point of departure.

Inspirational rhythms

Such freedom crossed stylistic boundaries and had an influence on almost all musicians of the period. They realised that they were no longer bound by well-used repetitive forms and structures and began to operate in fresh, often simpler, ways. Davis took full advantage of this in the next few years in work with his new band, which included three of the musicians who became closely linked with the jazz-rock movement. For them, and many others, exposure to Miles Davis and his thinking had an inestimable effect. They were saxophonist Wayne Shorter (later to form Weather Report with Joe Zawinul), who provided many of the compositions, pianist

Right: Smoke gets in your eyes. From his early days with Charlie Parker (inset above), trumpeter Miles Davis (above) was constantly innovative, and his work had a great influence on many rock musicians.

Herbie Hancock and drummer Tony Williams.

Williams' rhythmic concept, in particular, added a lot to the group, now remembered as one of the best jazz outfits of all time. He played *around* the beat rather than stating it forcefully, and his superimpositions of double, triple and quadruple time over the basic pulse provided much of the group's excitement. One of the best examples of the group's approach to rhythm can be heard on the title track to *Nefertiti* (1968), where Davis and Shorter provide the basic structure with their repetitive playing of the theme, leaving the rhythm players to improvise freely.

All this music had been made on acoustic instruments: Hancock on the grand piano and Ron Carter, a superb player, on the traditional upright bass. However, in 1968 Davis started to use electric instruments, at first mainly for their colouristic possibilities; they eventually replaced the regular instruments on *Miles In The Sky* (1968) and *Filles De Kilimanjaro* (1968).

A silent way

For his next record, *In A Silent Way*,
recorded early in 1969, Davis augmented
his group with *three* keyboards – played by
Chick Corea, Herbie Hancock and Josef
Zawinul. Together with Tony Williams
and new bassist Dave Holland, they laid
down a filigree carpet of sound for solos
from Davis, Shorter and guitarist John
McLaughlin. Unusually for jazz at that
time, Davis had heavily edited the performances in the studio as well as repeat-
ing some of the sections. The album was
thus created as much after the session as
during it, and this outraged many diehard
Davis fans who preferred the 'truth' of a
live performance.

However, such fresh sounds attracted a
different, younger audience, many of
whom discovered Miles following a cover
feature in the December 1969 edition of
Rolling Stone and the publicity given to his
next album, *Bitches Brew* (1970). As with
In A Silent Way, many instruments were
used to create a background – this time
further enhanced by the burblings of
Bennie Maupin's bass clarinet – for
the solos of Davis, Shorter and
McLaughlin.

The success of Davis' controversial
new approach was evident; he was
selling records in quantities previously unknown to a jazz musician.
After some initial problems, he
began to play live concerts to rock
audiences, even topping the bill at
such venues as the Fillmore East.
Inevitably the band underwent several
changes, with Michael Henderson replacing Holland on bass and Keith Jarrett joining on keyboards. Drummer Billy Cobham
also spent some time with Davis, as did
percussionist Airto Moreira, drummer Al
Foster, saxophonist Dave Leibman and
guitarist Larry Coryell. Albums such as
Jack Johnson (1971), *Live Evil* (1972), *On
The Corner* (1973) and *Agharta* (1975)
were successful, but faced serious competition from those by Davis' alumni.

After those early Seventies albums,
Davis fell silent. Rumours inevitably
spread that 'something was happening',
that Miles would return at the end of the
decade – as he had done previously in the
Forties, Fifties and Sixties – with a brand
new direction to astound his fans. Sadly,
the reasons for his disappearance from the
music scene were the recurrence of an
earlier hip-joint problem and an ulcer
operation.

In the early Eighties, Davis began touring and recording again with a six-piece
band featuring Marcus Miller (bass), Bill
Evans (soprano sax), Mike Stern (guitar),
Al Foster (drums) and Mino Cinelu (percussion). By 1986's *Tutu*, Miller was sup-
plying all backing instruments, playing the
part of a modern Gil Evans but using synthesisers not strings. In 1988's *Siesta*, the
duo created a work critics were comparing
with the classic *Sketches Of Spain*.

GRAHAM COLLIER

Heavy Weather

Weather Report's high pressure improvisation

IT IS HARD TO BELIEVE that when the newly-formed Weather Report were rehearsing for the 1971 Newport Jazz Festival, they were pushed to find enough material for a full live set. With an album and a world tour each year in the ensuing decade, the two survivors of the original line-up, Josef Zawinul and Wayne Shorter, were faced in the Eighties with the problem of deciding what to include from their massive output. But in the summer of 1971 the venture seemed merely the customary case of that year's star jazzmen getting together for a recording session with whatever material was to hand.

Usually these *ad hoc* mixtures brought together by record companies produce albums of historical interest and technical virtuosity but very little magic. Weather Report, however, was different. Zawinul (born 7 July 1932) and Shorter (25 August 1933) had met when the former arrived from his native Austria. They had kept in touch while pursuing parallel courses – Zawinul with Maynard Ferguson, Yusef Lateef and Cannonball Adderley (whose pop-jazz hit 'Mercy, Mercy, Mercy' he wrote), and Shorter with Art Blakey's Jazz Messengers and Miles Davis. It was on the Miles Davis albums *In A Silent Way* (1969) – which took its title from a Zawinul composition – and *Bitches Brew* (1970) that the two finally came together to prepare the ground for their own group.

Sound pictures

The bassist they chose was Miroslav Vitous (born 6 December 1947), the Czech virtuoso who had stunned jazz fans and musicians with his playing with Stan Getz, Herbie Mann and others. His style was far removed from the plonking background accompaniment of the average jazz bassist – he amplified and treated the sound to give a growling, almost vocal line that stood shoulder-to-shoulder with the front-line instruments. It fitted well with the oblique approach favoured by both Zawinul on keyboards and Shorter on sax, hinting at the written notes then sliding off into melodic asides before suddenly pouncing on the theme again.

The first album, *Weather Report* (1971), showed to perfection the result of these three improvising together over a floating, tinkling carpet of rhythm laid down by drummer Alphonse Mouzon (born 21 November 1948) and Brazilian percussionist Airto Moreira (5 August 1941), who played the then obligatory battery of cuicas, caixixi, jawbones and all manner of devices. Vitous' bass and Shorter's soprano

sax wove unison duets; Zawinul's electric piano hinted at chords and the usually prominent solo instruments drifted in and out of the foreground in a laid-back, impressionistic manner.

For a couple of years this line-up continued, with Eric Gravatt and Dom Um Romao replacing the original percussionists. The second album, *I Sing The Body Electric* (1972), had one side studio-recorded and the other taken from a concert in Japan; the full, uncut version of the latter, released on Japanese CBS, showed that any hint of meandering was ruthlessly excised, even sections of only a few bars. The live side gives a great impression of the energy and fluency that developed as the band played more and more together. While Gravatt powered them all along, Zawinul took the Rhodes piano to its limits with all kinds of distortion effects, a hint of the synthesiser sound-empire he was to begin building soon after.

Heat waves

Then came the relative disappointment of the 1973 album *Sweetnighter*, on which the band sounded bored and unhappy by their previous standards of exuberance. The recording was dry and lifeless, the rhythm section sounded like a drum machine on autopilot and Zawinul as a composer was at his most minimal. Even accepting that the hip thing at that time was to sit back and groove, that it was bad form to write too much or have complicated structures, it was a sad album. The fact that Vitous was on his way out (his leaving card being the record's outstanding composition, 'Will') probably had much to do with that.

After various personnel changes, however, the band that visited Europe in 1973 brought renewed hope. Zawinul started using more synthesiser, both as a solo instrument and an occasional chord-filler and, by the time 1974's *Mysterious Traveller* appeared, Weather Report had regained both quality and imagination. It was on a different level, however – with this album they verged at times on the grandiose, employing canned applause, massed choirs of synthesisers and a lush Californian studio sound. At the same time they showed they had lost none of their intimacy, as the delicacy of Shorter's 'Blackthorn Rose' amply demonstrated. Their bassist for the next two years was Alphonso Johnson, loose-limbed and nimble, funky but imaginative.

The band's next album, *Tail Spinnin'* (1975), was an attractive, freewheeling showcase for Zawinul and Shorter's exemplary writing and playing. Then, in 1976, some of the best work they had ever recorded was released – the album *Black*

Market. Everything about it was excellent. It was both subtle and powerful, and it marked an invigorating return from an unvarying, jazz-funk, rhythm-machine feel to human, organic playing. Zawinul's lush use of synthesisers brought colour to

Below: Weather Report's Wayne Shorter sings the body electric on soprano saxophone. Flanked by Joe Zawinul on keyboards and Jaco Pastorius on bass (inset below), Shorter was a key member of the group.

the arrangements and everyone's playing was faultless. Two of the tracks, 'Cannon Ball' and 'Barbary Coast', featured the arrival of bassist Jaco Pastorius, whose 'singing' bass tone – achieved with the aid of his fretless Fender Jazz Bass – and unsurpassed dexterity were soon to bring him fame.

The triumvirate of Zawinul-Shorter-Pastorius continued until 1982, producing a series of albums that stood as models for the admittedly declining number of jazz-rock practitioners. Certain gems and nuggets shone out, like 1978's *Mr Gone* and the joyful 'Birdland' on its predecessor, *Heavy Weather* (1977), before Pastorius eventually went the way of previous Weather Report bassists.

By the Eighties, Weather Report had probably passed their peak, but were still out on their own in the field of jazz-rock. The original live spirit of 1971 had become enshrined: Zawinul now claimed the title of Orchestrator, and indeed many of the little riffs and phrases that he used to zip out as throwaways on the electric piano reappeared as written themes or arrangements, scored for several instruments.

By the time Pastorius died in a club fight in late 1987, the group had long since ceased to function   HUGH HOPPER

Weather Report
Recommended Listening

Weather Report (CBS 32024) (Includes: Milky Way, Umbrellas, Morning Lake, Tears, Waterfall, Eurydice); *Heavy Weather* (CBS 81775) (Includes: Birdland, A Remark You Made, Palladium, Havana, The Juggler, Teen Town).

THE LATIN QUARTER

Santana: percussive power and a singing guitar

EMERGING AT THE END of the Sixties from the heart of hippiedom, San Francisco's Haight-Ashbury area, Santana were the first band to find success with a merger of electric rock and the percussive rhythms of Central America and Africa. The band has had a chequered career since their inception, the one constant feature being the highly distinctive guitar-playing of Carlos Santana. However, despite continued activity and international success into the Eighties, it is their earlier work with its startling energy and successful fusion of musical forms that remains their most significant contribution to the history of rock.

The Cisco Kid

Carlos Santana, born in Mexico on 20 July 1947, was brought up in the town of Autlan de Novarra. His father, Jose Santana, was a Mariachi musician who emigrated with their family to San Francisco in 1962, but it wasn't until 1966 that the young Carlos joined them there. San Francisco was then a hot-bed of musical activity and innovation and Carlos, who had taken up guitar in 1961, lost no time in becoming involved. A mutual friend introduced him to Mike Bloomfield, with whom he sat in for a jam; guitarist Tom Frazier, who witnessed the session, was so impressed with Carlos' playing that he afterwards tracked down the Mexican and suggested that they start a band together. By the end of 1966, Santana and Frazier had recruited percussionist Mike Carabello and organist Gregg Rolie – the Santana Bluesband had been born. (Bloomfield was impressed, too, and later on, in 1968, invited the guitarist to join him and Al Kooper on stage at the Fillmore West – the results appeared on the 1969 album *Live Adventures Of Mike Bloomfield And Al Kooper*.)

It was at this early stage that Bill Graham, promoter of the hugely prestigious Fillmore venues, first became involved with the band. Having originally met Carlos trying to sneak into the Fillmore West through a toilet window, Graham gave the Bluesband work at the venue; among the bands they supported were Paul Butterfield and the Who. In a personnel shuffle around July 1967, founding member Tom Frazier left, while David Brown joined on bass and Marcus Malone was added on percussion. The band's name was shortened to Santana, and, largely due to Malone's influence, the music started to move away from its blues roots towards a more Afro-Cuban, percussively-dominated sound.

This trend continued when Latin percussionist Jose 'Chepito' Areas was recruited in July 1969. Marcus Malone was convicted on a charge of manslaughter in mid 1969 and departed to serve his jail sentence, leaving a line-up comprising Santana, Mike Carabello (percussion), David Brown (bass), Chepito Areas (percussion/trumpet), Mike Shrieve (drums), and Gregg Rolie (organ/vocals) to become the first unrecorded band to headline at the Fillmore West. They then took the stage at the celebrated Woodstock Festival in August 1969.

Santana's appearance at Woodstock launched them into rock's premier division without further ado, and when their debut album *Santana* was released on Columbia later that year, it very quickly became a million-seller. CBS producer David Rubinson recalls: 'When it came out, you could not turn on the radio for six weeks without hearing the damned record!' The group also appeared in the *Woodstock* film (1970) and their performance of 'Soul Sacrifice' remains one of the movie's highlights: a battery of Latin percussionists lined up behind the guitarist, his face grotesquely distorted in an effort to wring the last drop of emotion from his sweetly-singing guitar.

The film helped to introduce Santana to a wider audience; a second album, *Abraxas* (1970), quickly scaled the charts on both sides of the Atlantic, while a version of Fleetwood Mac's 'Black Magic Woman' afforded the group a Number 4 hit single in the US.

It is the first two albums with the six-piece line-up that constitute the most enduring of Santana's recorded work. Both records were highly distinctive and charged with an ethnic vitality quite unlike the more weighty and sombre heavy rock of that period. Drummer Mike Shrieve and bassist David Brown laid a steady but rolling foundation, while the twin percussion of Areas and Carabello added dynamic variety and rhythmic thrust, their contributions being especially enhanced by the unusually deft production that often placed them at either extreme of the stereo 'left-to-right' image. Gregg Rolie's organ and powerful soul vocals counterpointed Carlos Santana's extravagantly sustained and vibrant guitar work, to complete a melodically textured and explosively percussive sound. The quality of the songs was undeniable: standouts were *Santana*'s 'Soul Sacrifice' and 'Evil Ways' and *Abraxas*' 'Samba Pa Ti' (which made the UK Top Thirty when re-released as a single in 1974).

Devadip's devotion

Throughout 1971 various additional recruits joined the line-up; by the time the band came to record *Santana 3*, guitarist Neal Schon had brought his more technically complete, but also rather staid style to the group, while Coke Escovedo had joined to add further percussion. By this time, however, the drug habits of certain band members were causing disenchantment, mistrust and upheaval within the ranks. Following a drugs charge in August 1971, bassist David Brown left to be replaced by Tom Rutley and by the end of 1971 most of the band had split amid confusion and acrimony. Neal Schon and Gregg Rolie later went on to form the hugely successful Journey. Santana ceased to exist as a touring unit for the following nine months, although Carlos recorded the jazz-influenced *Caravanserai* album in 1972 with selected personnel.

The year 1972 saw Carlos Santana undergo a period of transition and re-assessment; he came to embrace the religious teachings of the guru Sri Chinmoy, later adopting the name Devadip Carlos Santana as a mark of his conversion. The move away from drugs towards religion seemed to strengthen the guitarist's resolve. His new band, put together in September 1972, retained only the services of percussionist Chepito Areas and drummer Mike Shrieve; newcomers included dis-

Above: Carlos Santana (second from left) with drummer Michael Shrieve (third from left) and the classic six-piece line-up of the late Sixties. Opposite: The sweet sustain of Santana's singing guitar.

Left: Carlos plays Gibson in the early Seventies. Above left: Chepito Areas (left) and Mingo Lewis add Latin percussion. Above: Santana in the Eighties, with David Margen (left) and Alex Ligertwood.

tinguished jazz vocalist Leon Thomas, keyboardist Tom Coster and percussionist Armando Peraza.

The musicians were now hired and paid a salary by Carlos, and it was even reported that he had instituted a system of fines for wrong notes and misconduct after the fashion of James Brown and Ray Charles. In 1975, Carlos explained his policy thus: 'The line-up only changes when things conflict. And it only conflicts with people when they're not being sincere and when they haven't a 100 per cent commitment to the band as far as not drinking and not taking drugs.'

As well as hiring and firing members of the endlessly changing Santana line-ups, Carlos also collaborated with the Mahavishnu Orchestra's John McLaughlin, the man who had introduced him to the teachings of Sri Chinmoy, to produce the woefully overblown *Love Devotion And Surrender* (1973), a compendium of rock-guitar bombast. *Welcome* (1973) continued the progression towards a more jazz-dominated fusion – the title track was a John Coltrane composition – and Leon Thomas's rich, muscular singing lent an air of authority to the album. It was the last to feature Santana's longest surviving collaborator, drummer Mike Shrieve, who fell ill on the eve of an American tour in August 1974 and was swiftly replaced. A brilliant and steadfast player throughout Santana's trying history, Shrieve nonetheless left with the accusation from Carlos that 'He was getting wishy-washy on his drums.' He went on to form the anything but wishy-washy Automatic Man.

Santana's 1974 release, *Borboletta*, was also in the jazz-rock idiom but was both a critical and commercial disappointment, and it now became apparent that the band was beginning to lose its audience. The 1976 album *Amigos*, however, was a clear and commercially successful attempt to return to the old Santana's Latin roots. It

was also the first Santana album to reach the Top Ten in America since their third, back in 1971. *Festival* (1976) and the double *Moonflower* (1977) continued in this vein, the latter album yielding their biggest-ever British hit single, a remake of the Zombies' 'She's Not There', which reached Number 11 in 1977.

Whatever else his religion may have done, it seems to have kept Carlos Santana in good shape. He worked without respite throughout the Seventies and, as well as touring and recording with Santana, contributed to albums by Narada Michael Walden and Herbie Hancock, and produced a solo album *Oneness/Silver Dreams Golden Reality* (1979). In the late Seventies Santana flirted with the disco/soul fusion rhythms of the city dancefloor – on *Inner Secrets* (1978) and *Marathon* (1979) – before returning once again to a more traditional formula on *Zebop!* (1981) and *Shango* (1982).

By now, the Santana band had become entirely a vehicle for the grimacing guitarist who once described his ever-changing group as: 'An institution flowing through time and space. Musicians come into the flowing river, ride through the rapids into calmer water and then move on to be replaced by others who add their own energy and inspiration to its flow.'

While there has never been another band quite like Santana, there can be no doubting their influence in alerting many rock and soul bands to the possibilities of using percussion to embellish their music. Their approach can be seen to have percolated through to such diverse artists as Sly Stone, Talking Heads, Pigbag, and many other bands who have been inspired to utilise a varied assortment of percussive devices as part of a propulsive rhythmic attack.   DAVID SINCLAIR

Santana
Recommended Listening

Santana (CBS 63815) (Includes: Evil Ways, Soul Sacrifice, Waiting, Shades Of Time, Savor, Jin-Go-Lo-Ba); *Abraxas* (CBS 64087) (Includes: Black Magic Woman/Gypsy Queen, Crying Beasts, Samba Pa Ti, Oye Como Va, Incident At Neshabur, El Nicoya).

BLOOD, SWEAT AND TEARS

The band that put brass into Sixties rock

BS&T in 1972. Clockwise, from left: Jerry Fisher, Bobby Colomby, Dave Bargeron, Jim Fielder, Larry Willis, Lou Marini, George Wadinius, Steve Katz, Lou Soloff and Chuck Winfield.

TIME HAS NOT been kind to Blood, Sweat and Tears. They are either remembered for the extravagance and musical pretentiousness of that brief period during 1970-71 when they were one of the world's leading rock acts, or for the commercial and artistic enfeeblement of later years. They tend not to be remembered for their exciting and innovative work of the late Sixties. Although reviled ever since by the critics and spurned by the public, in the Sixties the group had credibility-plus. After all, it had been founded by Al Kooper, whose own personal standing had been high from the time he'd first attracted attention as one of Bob Dylan's sidemen between 1965 and 1966 during the latter's *Highway 61/ Blonde On Blonde* period. Kooper had then gone on to form Blues Project, a band that had won great critical acclaim as *the* outstanding East Coast blues outfit.

In May 1967 Kooper left Blues Project and travelled throughout the US searching for recruits for a new band. In the event he only discovered bass-player Jim Fielder, who had previously had brief engagements with Frank Zappa's Mothers of Invention and Buffalo Springfield. Kooper decided to continue his search in London, but lacked the financial means of getting there. To pay his fare, he agreed to do some solo gigs at the Café Au-Go-Go in Greenwich Village, where Blues Project had first cut their teeth. His backing musicians were Fielder on bass, Steve Katz (a former ex-Blues Project member) on guitar and Bobby Colomby on drums.

Kooper became so enthusiastic about this line-up that he scrapped his London plans. Instead he recruited a four-man horn section: Fred Lipsius, Randy Brecker, Dick Halligan and Jerry Weiss. Blood, Sweat and Tears were thus intended from the start to employ a horn section as an integral part of their sound.

Classic rockers

The line-up contained some highly-trained musicians, some of whom had academic qualifications in music, and thus reflected the fact that the rock music of that period was becoming more and more sophisticated. While Kooper – who freely admitted that his own organ-playing was rudimentary – was still around, the group was able to maintain the delicate balance between technical ability and the untutored exploration that is so essential to rock.

Child Is Father To The Man (1968) was an excellent debut album – it was well-conceived, containing versions of songs by composers such as Randy Newman and Carole King, and enjoyable to listen to. Kooper's concept was simply to use horns to achieve a fuller sound in order to diversify and broaden the range of rock. The album featured ambitious horn arrangements in the tradition of jazz trumpeter Maynard Ferguson (whom Kooper cited as an important influence), and was genuinely innovatory.

By the time of 1969's self-titled second album, however, the band had lost Kooper,

Top: Vocalist David Clayton-Thomas (left) leads the refrain. Above: Al Kooper rehearses the group's original brass section, from left Fred Lipsius, Dick Halligan, Jerry Weiss and Randy Brecker.

who moved on to other work, notably the *Super Session* project with Mike Bloomfield and Stephen Stills. If he felt that the band he'd created was capable of looking after itself, he'd have been correct.

A changed line-up was thus responsible for *Blood, Sweat And Tears* and the band's third album, *Blood, Sweat And Tears 3* (1970), which together catapulted the band into the superstar league. Brecker and Weiss had left in Kooper's wake, the former to become a much sought-after sessioneer. The departing trio had been replaced by four newcomers: Chuck Winfield (trumpet, flugelhorn), Lew Soloff (trumpet, flugelhorn, piano), Jerry Hyman (trumpet), and last but not least vocalist David Clayton-Thomas. Born in London on 13 September 1941 and a naturalised Canadian, Clayton-Thomas had a massive frame to match a massive voice; his reputation rocketed with that of the group.

Ambassadors of the arts

Blood, Sweat And Tears topped the US charts in the spring months of 1969. It yielded three major hit singles – Laura Nyro's 'And When I Die', the old Motown chestnut 'You Made Me So Very Happy' by Brenda Holloway and Clayton-Thomas' own 'Spinning Wheel'. Although it was a powerful and positive album, it also revealed the group becoming more self-consciously arty and less in touch with its rock roots. Suddenly, the band's audience, however numerous, seemed overwhelmingly composed of young, well-dressed business executives. It might almost be said that Blood, Sweat and Tears were appealing to an audience that didn't like rock music. Their identification with the establishment seemed complete when they undertook a tour of Iron Curtain countries (Yugoslavia, Rumania and Poland) in the summer of 1970 on behalf of the US State Department.

This process became even more pronounced on *Blood, Sweat And Tears 3*, when the group tried both to repeat a successful formula (this time without the producer of their inspired second album,

James William Guercio, who had left to shape Chicago's career) and to continue moving in the direction of 'art'. Where they had once been enjoyable and imaginative, they now became ponderous.

The album contained hit singles, most notably the Clayton-Thomas composition, 'Lucretia MacEvil', and there were also lengthy versions of two popular rock songs – the Rolling Stones' 'Sympathy For The Devil' and Traffic's '40,000 Headmen', both of which had been extended to incorporate 'classical' interludes. Rock fans hated such treatments, and regarded the group with something close to open hostility, while previously sympathetic rock critics turned on them savagely.

This adverse reaction gradually gained momentum from the summer of 1970 onwards, when the group, having just returned from Eastern Europe, achieved their second consecutive US Number 1 album with *Blood, Sweat And Tears 3*. So popular were they in concert at that time that Clayton-Thomas was moved to observe that 'There are only 20 cities in the

Blood, Sweat and Tears are shed on stage by the band at the height of their career in the late Sixties. From 1970 onwards, it was downhill all the way.

US with big enough concert halls for us to play.' Yet suddenly the bubble burst, and Blood, Sweat and Tears abruptly found themselves the most unfashionable of outfits. Some group members felt this keenly and accordingly tried to retrace their steps, consciously moving back towards rock at the expense of the band's proven formula. In addition to the unsettling effect of a lack of critical respectability, the group's other main problem was the total absence of a guiding personality. In 1971, Clayton-Thomas left to pursue a solo career; although he returned 18 months later, his presence was insufficient to revive the band's fortunes.

Blood, Sweat and Tears shifted an incredible 35 million records for CBS, mostly in their peak years between 1969 and 1971; since 1972, they hardly sold anything, and a label change to ABC (later MCA) availed them nothing. After their commercial star had waned, their biggest mistake was simply to have kept going. By 1980 this once-proud band was in the humiliating position of being forced to cancel UK appearances because of a complete lack of interest on the part of audiences; Blood, Sweat and Tears still had trouble finding somewhere to play – somewhere small enough.   BOB WOFFINDEN

Blood, Sweat and Tears
Recommended listening

Blood, Sweat and Tears (CBS 63504) (Includes: And When I Die, Spinning Wheel, You Made Me So Very Happy, Smiling Phases, More And More).

New Pioneers

The early Seventies saw US music getting back to the roots

THE TURN OF the Sixties in the US saw a period where the pigeonholing of rock music and musicians became fashionable; journalists coined an array of shorthand categories with dubious accuracy and astonishing rapidity, like folk- and country-rock (which stuck) or raga- and space-rock (which sounded downright contrived). *Time*'s 1970 cover article on the Band proclaimed them 'The New Sound of Country Rock' with some justification (before they outgrew the label) and Gram Parsons was one of that genre's leading lights, but Tim Buckley, Ry Cooder and Van Morrison rendered any such categorisation obsolete.

Those musicians all came from very varied backgrounds, but all showed themselves to be of lasting influence. With the exception of Parsons, they were city boys, sharing their

Above: 'Getting it together in the country' – a crucial part of the hippie lifestyle – was wholeheartedly embraced by Van Morrison (pictured with his wife Janet Planet) when resident in Woodstock.

basic inspirations of rock'n'roll, R&B, country music and blues from which they created vital new music. They also acknowledged those abiding influences; witness Van Morrison's soulful rendition of Willie Dixon's 'I Just Want To Make Love To You' on 1974's *It's Too Late To Stop Now*, the Band's choice of Muddy Waters as a guest for *The Last Waltz* in 1976, and Cooder's resurrection of 'Little Sister', originally an Elvis Presley hit, in 1979.

A trend in the Sixties was the formation of centres with distinctive community spirits. Some were the target of arbitrary press attention, such as Swinging London or San Francisco. Others were spared such a fate and became true communities, rather than media-appointed scenes, thereby avoiding the 'launching pad' aura of places like London or

Nashville. But it was not always possible to escape the public eye completely. Much to the displeasure of its residents, Woodstock's image was tarnished in 1969 by the Woodstock Music and Art Fair with which the township was linked in the public imagination, although its origins were far removed from the hugely successful *Woodstock* package. In 1901, expatriate Englishman Ralph Whitehead's search for a place to settle and establish a colony for artists and artisans came to an end. His vision, realised in the Catskills, became, in time, the home base of artists like Raoul Hague or a refuge for 'tourists' like avant-garde classical composer John Cage.

By the late Sixties a thriving community of musicians had congregated there, many of whom had turned their backs on the hubbub of the Big Apple, some 100 miles distant. Van Morrison, for example, had been inveigled to New York City by Bert Berns and rented a house in Woodstock; in time, the throng included John Simon, Happy and Artie Traum, John Sebastian, Bob Dylan, Paul Butterfield, Geoff and Maria Muldaur and, of course, the Band. On the sleeve of their 1968 debut album, *Music From Big Pink*, the Band paid homage to 'a pink house seated in the sun of Overlook Mountain in West Saugerties', while their family portrait reinforced family ties in an era when youth rebellion against the older generation's values and mores was the prevailing trend. Between June and October 1967, Big Pink additionally gave birth to Dylan's *Basement Tapes*, and it was Dylan's retreat to the relative solitude of 'his mountain hideaway', as the *New York Daily News* described it, after 'the motorcycle accident that almost cost him his life' that gave Woodstock the royal seal of approval. In time many of its intake departed, but that environment helped inspire *Moondance, John Wesley Harding* and *The Band*. If further testimony were required, the Band's *The Last Waltz* neatly encapsulated much of that era on celluloid from the standpoint of the Seventies.

Down in Hollywood
Los Angeles typified a diametric opposite to the Woodstock idyll. Not only was its climate an utter contrast, but the attitudes of its citizens were poles apart. In the mid to late Sixties, LA had been the stamping ground of the Byrds, the Nitty Gritty Dirt Band, Love, the Mothers Of Invention *et al*, with no single, cohesive style gaining the whip hand. It was a city of *possibilities*, something which acted as a strong lure, 'a futuristic place' as Ry Cooder described it. The city clearly exerted a powerful attraction for musicians in the Seventies onwards. Tim Buckley, born in Amsterdam, NY, based himself there, even jokingly calling an album *Greetings From LA*; his sense of the absurd also encompassed a cameo appearance in the Monkees' TV show.

Two bands that exemplified the richness of the American rock tradition were the Flying Burrito Brothers (top) and the Band (left). Each created a unique blend of rock'n'roll, country and R&B. Tim Buckley (opposite) started out as a folk singer but soon began to investigate jazz and funk.

Gram Parsons, too, went out west and fused his Southern upbringing and country music influences with the lonesome LA cowboy ways to produce a masterpiece in *Gilded Palace Of Sin* (1969). 'This old town's filled with sin, it'll swallow you in,' sang the Burritos in 'Sin City'; it was every country boy's lament. Parsons' acuity also fuelled the Stones' vision, spotlit in 'Wild Horses' and 'Dead Flowers'. Cooder pinpointed LA's significance: 'Every kind of musician lives there . . . so you have opportunities to do what you want to do. Record studios. Musicians. Hell! I can organise a session in five minutes on the telephone, get in there and do whatever you want to do.' Although very much the product of LA's thriving session scene, Cooder was one of a handful of session men who have launched successful solo careers in their own right.

City sounds
One thing that neither Woodstock nor LA created was a truly regional music akin to the regionalism found in the formative days of rock'n'roll, whether 'Memphis sound' or Merseybeat. If an LA sound existed, it was as a result of superbly crafted accompaniments by a select bunch of studio musicians producing bland, FM-oriented music. Radio was a crucial element in the careers of Buckley, Morrison and the others, for it coincided with the rise of a new radio format. Hitherto American radio stations playing rock music, as opposed to ones focusing on regional, ethnic, specialist or highbrow music, would programme around the Top Forty, spiced with liberal doses of jingles and adverts.

The stations were loath to tamper with the formula, but change was on the way. The popularity, availability and increasing sophistication of hi-fi equipment, coupled with the ascent of LP sales, foreshadowed a change and existing radio formats were unsuitable to cope with these phenomena. Commenting in 1967 in *Rolling Stone*, pioneering DJ Tom Donahue of KMPX-FM called Top Forty radio 'the biggest deterrent to the progress, expansion and success of contemporary music'. Donahue then proceeded to 'turn the world upside down' by programming LP cuts and whatever else took his fancy, irrespective of saleability in Top Forty terms.

By the Eighties, Tim Buckley and Gram Parsons had become rock'n'roll casualties, while the Band had split. Ry Cooder had progressed in status from cult hero to fully-fledged rock star, and Van Morrison – despite a two-year period of retirement in the mid Seventies – was still producing an uncompromising blend of melody and mysticism. Although largely eclipsed in commercial terms by those who followed them onto the FM airwaves – including the Eagles, Fleetwood Mac, the Doobie Brothers and Steely Dan – the music of these pioneering artists still remained landmarks in the constantly changing face of American rock music.

KEN HUNT

ROCK '72

While the 'progressive' rock groups of the late Sixties and early Seventies stimulated many with their emphasis on musical virtuosity, their live performances were seldom visually exciting experiences. 1972, however, brought with it a trend towards more theatrical and colourful presentation with the arrival of such artists as David Bowie and Alice Cooper.

Cooper had scored in the US in 1971 with 'Eighteen', but it wasn't until the following year's million-selling 'School's Out' that his lurid and macabre *grand guignol* came to international attention. David Bowie, meanwhile, had been recording since the mid Sixties, but it was his 1972 *Ziggy Stardust* album, and the extravagantly theatrical stage show that went with it, that propelled him to star status. Newcomers Roxy Music also sprang to prominence with their art-school camp and stylishness, while the New York Dolls hit Britain with their 'subterranean sleazoid flash'.

In America, however, softer, 'laid-back' sounds remained the prevailing rock trend. The Eagles, Jackson Browne and Loggins and Messina all released successful debut albums, Don McLean's 'American Pie' and 'Vincent' both sold a million while the temporary disbandment of Crosby, Stills, Nash and Young left a gap for America to fill.

January

4 The three-record set *Concert For Bangla Desh* by George Harrison and friends is awarded gold status just one month after its US release.
16 Schoolboy Neil Reid enters the UK Top Ten with the sentimental ballad 'Mother Of Mine'; the juvenile vocalist had one further (minor) hit before disappearing into obscurity.
David Seville, creator of the chart-topping novelty 'group' the Chipmunks, dies at the age of 52.
22 The New Seekers top the UK charts with 'I'd Like To Teach The World To Sing'; the song was originally an advertising jingle called 'I'd Like To Buy The World A Coke' recorded by the Hillside Singers.

February

14 John and Yoko start a week as hosts on the US chat show, *The Mike Douglas Chat Show.*
16 Paul McCartney and Wings make a surprise debut live performance at Nottingham University.
22 David Bowie, whose *Hunky Dory* LP was released the previous month, tells the press: 'I'm going to be huge – it's quite frightening.'
26 The BBC ban Wings' debut single 'Give Ireland Back To The Irish' on political grounds.

1972 – a good year for juveniles like Neil Reid (top right) and Donny Osmond (above right). Below: Album debutants Loggins and Messina. Opposite: Alice Cooper and friend.

March

11 Nilsson's 'Without You', written by Badfinger's Pete Ham and Tom Evans, reaches the top of the UK charts.
15 Trevor Howell, who attacked Frank Zappa at London's Rainbow Theatre the previous December, is sentenced to 12 months' imprisonment at the Old Bailey.
27 Jethro Tull and Grand Funk Railroad are barred from appearing at the Community Centre, Tucson, Arizona, on the grounds that they 'encourage the use of drugs'.

April

9 Sly Stone arrives at New York's Apollo Theatre for a Family Stone performance; the singer fails to appear on stage, however, preferring to remain in his dressing room watching TV.
15 'Amazing Grace', performed by the Pipe and Drums and Military Band of the Royal Scots Dragoon Guards and featuring a bagpipes solo by Pipe Major Tony Crease, tops the UK charts and goes on to become Britain's best-selling single of the year.
Dan Hicks and his Hot Licks are arrested for possession of marijuana during a performance at LA's Troubador.
16 The Electric Light Orchestra make their first live appearance in Croydon.
22 The management of the Royal Albert Hall announce that the venue will no longer host rock concerts because of an increasing 'hooligan element'.

May

5 Blues singer/guitarist the Reverend Gary Davis dies of a heart attack in New Jersey at the age of 72.

6 Todd Rundgren enters the US Top 40 with 'I Saw The Light'. The talented guitarist manages a dual career, playing with his band Utopia as well as making solo records.

10 Les Harvey, guitarist of Stone The Crows, is fatally electrocuted on stage at the Top Rank Suite, Swansea.

June

3 Blues singer 'Mississippi' Fred McDowell dies aged 68.

17 Jimmy McCullough, one-time guitarist with Thunderclap Newman, replaces the late Les Harvey in Stone The Crows.

July

1 Delaney and Bonnie Bramlett split up both maritally and professionally.

16 Smokey Robinson and the Miracles play their last date before Smokey departs, in Washington D.C.

17 A bomb explodes under a truckload of the Rolling Stones stage equipment in Montreal. No one is hurt but the PA system is seriously damaged.

25 Bobby Ramirez, drummer of Edgar Winter's White Trash, is savagely attacked outside a Chicago nightclub and receives fatal stab wounds.

August

2 Brian Cole, bass player and founder member of the Association, dies from a heroin overdose at his home in Gaelic Park, New York.

The five original Byrds, Roger McGuinn, David Crosby, Gene Clark, Michael Clarke and Chris Hillman, re-assemble in Los Angeles to record an album.

12 Alice Cooper's 'School's Out' replaces Donny Osmond's 'Puppy Love' at the top of the UK charts.

30 John Lennon and Yoko Ono perform at Madison Square Garden and are supported by Bobby Vinton, teen idol of the early Sixties.

September

8 The Gary Glitter single 'I Didn't Know I Loved You (Till I Saw You Rock'n'Roll)' is released in the UK. The song is later covered by Joan Jett and the Runaways.

16 Lieutenant Pigeon enter the UK charts with 'Mouldy Old Dough', a bouncy novelty instrumental featuring the jangling piano of Mrs Fletcher.

26 Jefferson Airplane's Grace Slick, Jack Casady and Paul Kantner are arrested and charged with assaulting a police officer following a gig at the Rubber Bowl, Akron, Ohio.

27 Rory Storm, of Liverpool group Rory Storm and the Hurricanes (from whom the Beatles poached Ringo Starr in 1962), takes a fatal overdose of sleeping pills.

October

13 Jazz-rock drummer Phil Seaman dies at his Lambeth home, aged 46.

14 Michael Jackson tops the US singles charts with 'Ben', the title song of a film about a rat.

25 Creedence Clearwater Revival disband.

29 The Osmonds arrive in London to appear at the Royal Variety Performance.

November

3 Singer-songwriting lovebirds James Taylor and Carly Simon are married in Manhattan.

6 Billy Murcia, drummer with the New York Dolls, dies in London following a night of excess at the Speakeasy club.

11 Berry Oakley, the Allman Brothers Band's bass player, dies in Macon, Georgia after crashing his motorcycle; Duane Allman had died similarly a year before.

18 Miss Christine of the GTOs and cover-girl of Frank Zappa's *Hot Rats* LP dies in Los Angeles from a heroin overdose at the age of 24.

Danny Whitten of Crazy Horse and composer of 'I Don't Want To Talk About It' (a Number 1 hit for Rod Stewart in 1977) dies from a heroin overdose.

December

2 The BBC ban Wings' new single 'Hi Hi Hi' because of its suggestive lyric. Chuck Berry is at Number 1 in the UK with the vulgar novelty song 'My Ding-A-Ling'.

9 Filming commences on *Pat Garrett And Billy The Kid*, directed by Sam Peckinpah and starring Kris Kristofferson and Bob Dylan.

23 Osmond family members have three records in the UK Top Ten: the Osmonds' 'Crazy Horses' (Number 5), Donny's 'Why' (Number 9) and Little Jimmy's 'Long Haired Lover From Liverpool' (Number 1).

TOM HIBBERT, JENNY DAWSON

BEST IN THE LAND

The Band's hymns to rural America

INSPIRED BY the dexterity of Ricky Nelson's legendary guitarist James Burton, and by Lonnie Mack, the young Robbie Robertson needed little incentive to join up with Ronnie Hawkins and take his first, unassuming steps along a road that led to him becoming part of what was arguably the finest American rock'n'roll band ever heard: the Band, *the* band.

Hawkins was a great bear of a man, a bar-room bawler from Arkansas who claimed to have made the first ever rockabilly record, a version of 'Bo Diddley'. As well as having worked in the cotton fields with Diddley, the loquacious Hawkins claimed he passed up the chance to record 'It's Only Make Believe' in favour of his friend Conway Twitty. No doubt these missed opportunities denied him what he considered his God-given right to succeed Elvis Presley as the King of rock'n'roll. Hawkins' response was to move to Canada in the late Fifties, taking with him a young drummer, Levon Helm (born in Arkansas in 1935).

Rockabilly roots

In Canada Hawkins had the audacity to call himself 'The King of Rockabilly'; but to make a living – always Hawkins' prime motive – he needed back-up musicians. Toronto in the early Sixties was pretty much like any other major city in the English-speaking world – twisting itself into a beat boom frenzy. Guitarist Jaime Robbie Robertson (born 1943), pianist Richard Manuel (born 1943), bass player Rick Danko (born 1942) and organist Garth Hudson (born 1937) had all been in high school bands during that first flush of youthful exuberance. Their groups had names like the Robots, Paul London and the Captors and Thumper and the Trombones, but as Hawkins and Helm gathered them up one by one, they became simply the Hawks.

As Ronnie Hawkins and the Hawks, they played their way around the bars and ballrooms of Canada and North America, mainly the Eastern Seaboard, grinding out Hawkins' unsubtle brew of Chuck Berry, Gene Vincent, Larry Williams and Bo Diddley fare. Hawkins himself was an undistinguished singer and harp-player, his main attraction being a high-pitched wail which Robertson would foil with piercing, angry guitar runs. The group made a few, rather ordinary records with Hawkins, but during sessions for his 1964 *Mojo Man* album, Levon Helm took over the microphone for stirring versions of Bobby Bland's 'Further On Up The Road' and Muddy Waters' 'She's 19'. Shortly afterwards, Helm felt confident enough to take the band out from under Hawkins and off

Opposite: The Band, from left: Rick Danko, Levon Helm, Richard Manuel, Garth Hudson and Robbie Robertson.

they went as Levon Helm and the Hawks.

Just what distinguished their music after only a few years together was a distillation of Americana that would gather both momentum and might in later years, the product of their reverence for the great black musicians of the Fifties.

Helm, meanwhile, gave voice to the new vision that Robertson was building for himself and the band. A drummer of unequivocal clout, Helm's vocals could send shivers up the spine. Though no songwriter himself, Helm was a powerful presence in a band with three distinctive vocalists, the others being Rick Danko and Richard Manuel. With each shabby jukejoint they played, sometimes under such names as the Crackers or the Canadian Squires, Levon and the Hawks meshed themselves a little closer musically, honing their technical prowess to the point where it looked and sounded so easy that it was surely lost on their audiences of 'pimps, rounders and flakeouts', as Garth once put it.

Levon and the Hawks cut but a few singles in those early days, mostly in small studios for small labels and nothing to set the world on fire, yet by 1965 they were somehow starting to garner a cult following on America's East Coast. Perhaps then, it wasn't surprising that the paradigm of Sixties cultists, Bob Dylan, heard the word on this dishevelled-looking bunch of Canadian rockers who *didn't* play Stones or Beatles re-hashes. As soon as Dylan saw them play, he knew they were the group he wanted to help him complete his transition from folk to rock.

Unannounced in their own right on Dylan's controversial 1965 and 1966 'electric' tours, the Hawks had become simply Bob Dylan's backing band; eclipsed as the star of the show, Levon left temporarily, to be replaced by Mickey Jones. Of those rancorous receptions, Robertson said: 'You get in this private plane, they fly you to this town, you play your music and people boo you. Then you get back on the plane, fly to another town, play the music and they boo you again . . . it was a strange way to make a living.'

Galling it may have been for the erstwhile Hawks, but in watching Dylan's metamorphosis from quasi-political folkie to awkward rock'n'roll star, they had been part of a unique phenomenon in a world dominated by nicely-packaged pop'n'roll. As this era drew to an end, the band found themselves back in an America exploding in a welter of musical self-recrimination. Unlike the majority of bands on the US scene at that time, the erstwhile Hawks were not politicians, polemicists or musical opportunists – and, perhaps most significantly, they were not Americans. They came from the cold insularity of Canada and had become stimulated by a country that was edgy, brash, yet somehow uncertain of itself and engagingly simple in its emotional character. In America they discovered the joys of jazz, gospel, country and western, blues and rock'n'roll music.

Sequestering themselves up in Woodstock, following Dylan's near-fatal motorcycle accident and after six years on the road, they at last had time to reflect on both the consequences of these influences on their music, as well as the dramatic shifts in their fortunes which now seemed to offer them a way out of the cul-de-sac of the barrelhouse circuit.

Pink mythology

'Being able to chop wood, fix the screen door and stuff was part of a life-style we happened to love,' explained Hudson in the slow-measured drawl that he shared with his four colleagues. 'We seemed to get a whole lot more [music] done when we didn't have a lot of company.' This may have sounded like the original justification for that hoary old rock-star apologia of 'getting it together in the country', but in the Band's case the result of those Woodstock months, playing with Dylan and one another, was one of the most remarkable albums of that, or indeed any other decade – *Music From Big Pink* (1968), named after the ugly but fondly-remembered house they all shared together.

As Greil Marcus eloquently said of that record in his book *Mystery Train*: 'Against a cult of youth they felt for a continuity of generations; against the instant America of the Sixties they looked for the traditions that made new things not only possible, but valuable. Against the pop scene, all flux and novelty, they set themselves; a band with years behind it, and meant to last.'

Explaining the musical motives a little more directly, Robertson later said, 'I can write about things that I can feel, something that I can relate to. It's not because I want to live there or anything, it's just storytelling. I could relate to farmers in the depression getting together in unions better than I could relate to if you want to go to San Francisco put a flower in your hair.'

Everything the group knew about music and playing it found a place in *Big Pink*, and without pomp or indeed any *direct* oratory, Robbie Robertson's songs (and those co-written by Dylan, Danko and Manuel) made an evocative statement about the 'lost' America they sought to rediscover.

The album started with Dylan and Manuel's 'Tears Of Rage', a tortured, even frightening dirge of brooding, loneliness and despair in a man who feels shut out, a metaphor for an America betrayed by those who somehow felt ashamed of it. In 'To Kingdom Come', the song that followed, this lost soul has all but given up and waits for death to come and relieve him of his grief; but it never does, and he is left to make something of his life, like it or not. The other songs on *Big Pink* are no less emotive; they were, in the main uptempo, and at times positively uplifting. 'We Can Talk About It Now', 'The Weight' and 'Chest Fever', with Hudson's majestic pipe-organ intro, were especially inspired.

The arrangements of these songs cast all manner of instruments, styles and musical filigree into what might have ended up as an over-ambitious conflict, were not the artists concerned so accomplished or familiar with one another's playing. Shreds of organ, piano or violin turned up in unexpected places, Robertson's guitar danced and dashed in and out with the grace of a ballet dancer but the impact of a meat cleaver.

Perhaps because they were primed by the group's association with Bob Dylan (who provided the album's cover artwork), *Big Pink* was an instant but well-deserved success. The follow-up LP, *The Band* (1969), confirmed both the group's brilliance and the enormous strength and maturity of Robertson's songwriting. *The Band* (1969) was even more of a musical exploration of the attitudes and legacies of America than its predecessor. From the Civil War ballad 'The Night They Drove Old Dixie Down' to the wry humour of 'Up On Cripple Creek', from the anger of 'Look Out Cleveland' to the beauty and pathos of 'Unfaithful Servant', the songs were written from the viewpoint of working-class middle Americans and poor Southerners and were perfectly complimented by understated playing and imaginative arrangements.

The album put the Band into the forefront of rock. Although their subsequent albums didn't always have the consistent quality of songwriting evident on *Big Pink* and *The Band*, they were always immaculately crafted. *Stage Fright* (1970) and *Cahoots* (1971) carried on the traditional themes of the first two LPs, while *Rock Of Ages* was a double live set recorded on 31 December 1971 at the New York Academy of Music. The sixth album, *Moondog Matinee* (1973), meanwhile, was a collection of pure rock'n'roll standards.

The last waltz

What almost all their work shared was a recognition of experience that the group invited their audience to participate in. Whether it was the sharecropper's lament of dashed fortunes and hopes for better times ahead in 'King Harvest Has Surely Come' (from *The Band*) or the ebullient, yet slightly desperate optimism of 'Life Is A Carnival' (from *Cahoots*), the Band could tap a nerve and inject into it an emotion or an attitude that was peculiarly American, the legacies of a young country growing up fast and making mistakes. Vocals that were alternatively plaintive and joyful perfectly expressed these qualities, while the music itself carried its own evocative synthesis of traditions.

Ultimately of course, the Band could have taken their folksy portraits of displacement and celebration to the cabaret circuit, maybe osmosing gently into country and western atrophy, but the disappointing *Northern Lights – Southern Cross* (1975) gave signs that inspiration was fading. After 16 years on the road – they had started touring again after *Big Pink* – the Band took the bold step of splitting up at the height of their career. On Thanksgiving Day in 1976, Bill Graham filled San Francisco's Winterland Ballroom with tables and chairs and served up turkey, cornbread and all the trimmings of this uniquely American festival. And, after 5000 fans had been fed, the curtains drew back and the Band played on for the last time, the event recorded by director Martin Scorsese's film cameras.

The Last Waltz, the film that documents this historic evening, adequately confirmed every lick of praise heaped on these five musicians.

In 1977, the Band issued a final album, *Islands*, and went their separate ways. Robertson moved into production work and subsequently took up a parallel career as a film actor and director, while Helm and Danko put out promising solo albums in 1977 and 1978. But after *The Last Waltz*, none of the members achieved the success,

Above: Band on the patio. Right: The last waltz – Dylan joins Robertson and the Band on stage, Thanksgiving Day, 1976.

musically or in any other sense, that they garnered as a group. Not that they appeared to have any regrets, for as Robbie Robertson had said at the end of the film: 'There's not much left we can take from the road . . . and you can press your luck; the road has taken a lot of the great ones, Hank Williams, Buddy Holly, Otis Redding, Janis, Jimi Hendrix, Elvis . . . it's a god-damn impossible way of life. No question about it.'

This was brought home in 1986 when Richard Manuel hanged himself while on the road with the reformed Band (*sans* Robertson). The guitarist, meanwhile, had released his first, self-titled solo album in 1987 which earned press plaudits and sired a hit single 'Somewhere Down The Crazy River'.

MARK WILLIAMS

**The Band
Recommended Listening**

Music From Big Pink (Capitol ST2955) (Includes: Chest Fever, Tears Of Rage, The Weight, To Kingdom Come, Caledonia Mission, In A Station); *The Band* (Capitol EST132) (Includes: Rag Mama Rag, Jawbone, Up On Cripple Creek, Look Out Cleveland, Rockin' Chair, When You Awake, Unfaithful Servant).

THE BELFAST COWBOY

Van Morrison: in pursuit of Romantic visions

ROCK WRITERS, like all journalists, make their money from covering people who make the biggest headlines – and not necessarily those who make the best or most lasting music. As some artists have learned to manipulate the rock press to advantage, so there are also the minority who turn their backs, inviting critical disinterest as a result. One such is Van Morrison. Embittered by the treatment to which he was subjected by the music business after leaving Belfast as a teenager in the early Sixties with Them, he has thenceforth paid lipservice or less to commercial or promotional matters, concerning himself only with the music. Whether or not this singular dedication has heightened his musical efforts, it is certain that the achievements of two decades are as eloquent as his public pronouncements have been unenlightening.

Backstreet jive and jellyroll

Born George Ivan Morrison in Belfast on 31 August 1945, he grew up in the far from prosperous Northern Irish capital. There was a definite American flavour to the music heard in the household: his mother Violet had been a jazz singer, while his father George had an extensive collection of country and blues records. Van took up the guitar in his early teens, eventually rejecting it for the then much more fashionable saxophone. It was this instrument that was to be his passport to the outside world when he, like so many others, looked to leave his crumbling native city.

The young Morrison matured in rock music's time-honoured fashion – on the road, in Van's case as sax-player for the

Left: Van the Man still into the music in the Eighties and (inset) miming with Them in England in 1966, shortly before he left the group.

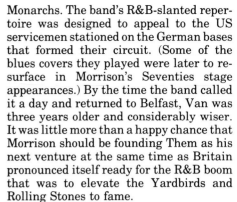

Monarchs. The band's R&B-slanted repertoire was designed to appeal to the US servicemen stationed on the German bases that formed their circuit. (Some of the blues covers they played were later to resurface in Morrison's Seventies stage appearances.) By the time the band called it a day and returned to Belfast, Van was three years older and considerably wiser. It was little more than a happy chance that Morrison should be founding Them as his next venture at the same time as Britain pronounced itself ready for the R&B boom that was to elevate the Yardbirds and Rolling Stones to fame.

Van has since stated that Them 'lived and died as a group on the stage of the Marine Hotel in Belfast'. Certainly, the band's short history was punctuated with innumerable personnel changes, while many of the later songs credited to the band heavily featured session musicians, much to the singer's disgust.

Chart success came early in 1965 with the band's second release; 'Baby Please Don't Go'/'Gloria' combined the A-side, a blues standard, with a Morrison original that displayed his already remarkable sense of dynamics.

The band had two further hits with 'Here Comes The Night' and 'Mystic Eyes' (a showcase for Morrison's storming harmonica work), but as Van gained in vocal assurance and left behind his stylistic debts to other R&B vocalists, Them were disintegrating. Their legacy was nine singles and a couple of albums (since endlessly repackaged), together with a handful of cover versions – Dylan's 'It's All Over Now Baby Blue' and Paul Simon's 'Richard Cory' – that hinted at their singer's growing authority.

Morrison's only ally, it seemed, was Bert Berns, writer/producer of 'Here Comes The Night' and something of a father figure. Berns' offer of an air ticket to New York opened a new chapter in the young Irishman's career, though it continued to be dogged by misfortune and manipulation. The recordings made with Berns were intended specifically for release as singles; 'Brown Eyed Girl' received deserved radio play. It was a summer anthem tailor-made for the airwaves and made the US Number 10 position in 1967. Many of the tracks were collected (without Morrison's consent) for release as *Blowin' Your Mind* (1967) and later reissued under at least three different titles – the first time in the very same year as the curiously mistitled *Best Of Van Morrison*. The singer was understandably disgruntled at what he saw as another piece of record business double-dealing and, wooed by Warner Brothers' promise of riches and a greater degree of artistic freedom, agreed to sign for the label after the death of Berns in late 1967.

The first fruits of the liaison, the album *Astral Weeks* (1968), represented a majestic advance on all Morrison's previously recorded work. Stylistically it combined R&B with jazz, folk and classical music, with an overall blues feel predominating. The instrumentation reflected this lush musical blend – to a basic rhythm section of upright bass, acoustic guitar and drums was variously added flute, brass, harpsichord, vibraphone and strings, the latter superbly arranged by Larry Fallon. The instruments bubbled beneath the surface of the mix or soared above it in complex dynamic interplay with Van's inspired vocal improvisations. The songs were ideal vehicles for the latter, being based around simple two or three-chord figures; any risk of resultant banality was eradicated by Morrison's astonishing lyrics which combined the directness of blues with images that owed much to Surrealism and British Romantic poetry.

Another time, another place

Astral Weeks also gave first utterance to the themes pervading and amplified by his subsequent work. Morrison projects himself both back to his Belfast childhood and forwards in time on a restless quest for the transcendence of spiritual anguish through a combination of sexual love and religious mysticism. The album's supreme achievement was 'Madame George', a lyrical evocation of childhood innocence that must be left behind. The song's simple structure was given a breathtaking lift by keening strings, in turn galvanised by Morrison's impassioned vocals.

Having got *Astral Weeks* out of his system, Morrison showcased the sunnier (and more commercial) side of his personality with *Moondance* (1970), which reflected the singer's move from the depressed backstreets of Belfast to the USA where, at least theoretically, all things were possible. The mood of the songs was carefree and optimistic, epitomised by the visionary 'Into The Mystic', in which Van imagined himself engaged with others on a joyous voyage of personal discovery – a theme that is crucial to his Romantic conceptions and constantly informs his work. Tight, funky brass arrangements replaced the melancholy strings of *Astral Weeks*.

The album displayed the breadth and depth of Morrison's songwriting, ranging from the jazzy Sinatra swing of the title cut to the punchy R&B of 'Caravan' and the gospel flavour of 'Brand New Day'. Among the musicians who were to enjoy a long relationship with Morrison to debut on *Moondance* included saxophonist Jack Schroer, keyboardist Jeff Labes and drummer Gary Mallaber.

Country roads

His status now assured, Van was free to explore the musical avenues suggested by his childhood listening – *His Band And Street Choir*, had its roots firmly in black music, while *Tupelo Honey* reflected the C&W influences imparted by Eddy Arnold and Jimmie Rodgers. Both released in 1971, they spawned US Top Thirty singles in 'Domino' and 'Wild Night' respectively: although critics demurred, enough people identified with *Tupelo Honey*'s gentle country love songs to ensure that it outsold not only its predecessors, but each of Morrison's well-received Seventies albums.

Marriage – to Janet Planet, whose picture on horseback adorned the cover of *Tupelo Honey* – had mellowed Morrison; in late 1971 they and daughter Shannon moved from Woodstock to Marin County, just north of San Francisco, where the couple had met after a Them gig in 1966.

Morrison gives it all he's got, backed by Pee Wee Ellis on tenor sax (below) and (above right) takes a turn on alto during a concert in Paris in 1974.

He resented the accusation – given weight by the record's packaging – that he had lost his edge, commenting 'a lot of people think that album covers are your life or something'. Sadly, the following year was to see their relationship end in divorce.

Despite such personal problems, 1972's *St Dominic's Preview* ended a fallow period by Morrison's self-imposed creative standards. Returning to the extended track format of *Astral Weeks* for the title cut, it featured another lengthy vocal and acoustic workout in 'Listen To The Lion'; once more the hypnotic combination of Morrison's pleading, throaty delivery and his simple, repetitive quasi-spiritual lyrics made for enthralling listening. He also threw a commercial single to the record moguls in 'Jackie Wilson Said (I'm In Heaven When You Smile)', a song revived in 1982 by Dexy's Midnight Runners with Morrison's approval.

Two talking points on the release of 1973's *Hard Nose The Highway* album were its surrealistic cover with its juxtaposition of Third World and Western images and the inclusion of 'Bein' Green', a song associated with Kermit the Frog from US TV's 'Sesame Street'. The jokey lyrics of 'Bein' Green' (the first cover version to surface on a Morrison solo album) spoke volumes. After reflecting that 'people tend to pass you over/Cos you're not standing out like flashy sparkles', Kermit finally decides that 'it'll do fine, it's beautiful/And I think it's what I want to be.' It seemed that Van Morrison would continue to go his own way regardless of outside influences.

In view of the repackaging of his Them and Bang label tracks, it was easy to understand Morrison's reluctance to issue a 'Best of' compilation. Nevertheless, *It's Too Late To Stop Now*, a live double album

recorded in LA and London in 1973, served the purpose well enough – the more so since both a horn and string section formed part of the Caledonia Soul Orchestra with which Morrison toured the US and Europe in that year; it comprised Dahaud Shaar (drums), Jeff Labes (piano), John Platania (guitar), David Hayes (bass), Jack Schroer (saxophone), Bill Atwood (trumpet), Nathan Rubin (violin) and Terry Adams (cello).

Mystic voyages
With its redefinition of his back catalogue, *Too Late* had marked the end of an era – a fact acknowledged by the title of Morrison's next but one album, *A Period Of Transition* (1977). In between came 1974's *Veedon Fleece*, his most introspective work since *Astral Weeks*, in which he retraced his Irish roots.

The years 1975-77 were spent in his native Ireland: Morrison confessed himself 'mentally exhausted'. Returning to the USA and recruiting Bill Graham as manager, Morrison followed the disappointing *A Period Of Transition* with *Wavelength* (1978). Its beguiling mix of chirpy, commercial melodies and sing-along lyrics helped it become his first US Top Thirty LP for five years.

Into The Music and *Common One*, released in 1979 and 1980 respectively, were relatively disappointing commercially, but showed that time had in no way dampened Morrison's spiritual fire, the singer employing his full vocabulary of vocal effects to put over complex images and ideas. Both albums were openly devotional in tone, *Into The Music* being concerned primarily with love relationships – most movingly in the case of 'Angeliou' and his cover of Tommy Edwards' 'It's All In The Game'. 'Summertime In England' was

the high-point of *Common One*, a celebration of the English countryside, spiritual and physical love, larded with references to poets such as Wordsworth and Coleridge 'smokin' by the lakeside'. These and his subsequent Eighties albums *Beautiful Vision* (1982) and *Inarticulate Speech Of The Heart* (1983) amply demonstrated Morrison's avowed commitment to explore music that acts as 'a healing force . . . a medicine.'

The mid Eighties saw him move folkwards on *A Sense Of Wonder* (1984), renounce Scientology in *No Guru, No Method, No Teacher* (1986), embrace jazz in *Poetics Champions Compose* (1987) and collaborate with Irish folk heroes the Chieftains to produce the uplifting *Irish Heartbeat* (1988). The result was a body of work that stood comparison with any of his contemporaries.

Much of the motivation behind Morrison's work remains a matter for speculation, inviting critics to brand him some kind of Celtic shaman. Morrison himself scorns such fantasies: 'The only reason journalists call me a mystic or a legend is because they can't think of anything else to write.' Legend or not, Van Morrison has always placed a premium on self-satisfaction; from being dictated to by record company moguls in the days of Them, he has since – to the continuing delight of his many fans – proved conclusively that he alone calls the tune.   MICHAEL HEATLEY

Van Morrison
Recommended Listening

Astral Weeks (Warner Brothers K46024) (Includes: Cyprus Avenue, Ballerina, Madame George, Slim Slow Slider, Beside You); *Common One* (Mercury 6302 021) (Includes: Summertime In England, Spirit, Haunts Of Ancient Peace, Satisfied, When Heart Is Open).

GOODBYE · A

Tim Buckley's invitation to the blues

TIM BUCKLEY was always a singer whose talent at any one time was greater than the categories in which he was placed, and a unique vocal stylist and innovator who could never be safely typecast. Born in Washington on 14 February 1947 and raised in New York, Buckley moved to Anaheim, California when he was ten and during his teens began to develop a range of vocal phrasing and delivery that were part influenced by his mother's predilection for the great traditional interpreters – Lena Horne, Nat 'King' Cole – and partly a result of listening to modal horn players like Eric Dolphy and Albert Ayler. These musicians were his consuming passion and, even as a teenager, Buckley was reaching out towards five octaves by imitating trumpet phrases. More eccentrically still, he strengthened his vocal chords by screaming at the top of his voice at the passing traffic.

Later, he played guitar and sang in a number of country bands along with Jim Fielder (subsequently bass-player with

Buffalo Springfield and Blood, Sweat and Tears) and, in 1966, was spotted by Frank Zappa's manager Herb Cohen who, impressed by his vocal style, offered him a management deal. Cohen persuaded Jac Holzman, boss of Elektra Records, to pay a visit to Hollywood's Troubador Club where Buckley was playing with guitarist Lee Underwood and conga player Carter C. C. Collins. Impressed, Holzman duly signed the young singer.

Blue afternoons

In October 1966, *Tim Buckley* was released. It was a remarkable debut album, the backing provided by Underwood, Fielder, Van Dyke Parks (piano) and Billy Mundi (drums) perfectly complementing the highly romantic compositions. Buckley's songs blended the poetry of his lyricist friend Larry Beckett with haunting melodies that were neither typically psychedelic nor purely folk. On 'Understand Your Man', his unique voice hovered sweetly above the jangling electric rock accompaniment, while on 'Song Slowly Sung', a lingering love anthem, the arrangement was the height of sympathetic simplicity.

On Buckley's second album, *Goodbye And Hello* (1967), producer Jerry Yester added some ambitiously baroque orchestral arrangements to tantalising effect. Such songs as 'Goodbye And Hello', a hymn to lost youth, 'Once I Was' with its haunting melodies and the mysterious 'Morning Glory' further revealed Buckley's talent. However, it was on *Happy/Sad* (1969), *Lorca* (1970) – named after the murdered Spanish poet García Lorca – and *Blue Afternoon* (1970) that Buckley's idiosyncratic, free-form style of singing was heard to better effect. *Blue Afternoon* and *Lorca*, in particular, saw him moving toward jazz with a sparse backing that allowed his voice room to manoeuvre and to experiment.

It was during this period that the influential rock columnist Lilian Roxon wrote of Buckley: 'Nothing in rock, folk-rock or anything else prepares you for a Tim Buckley album . . . there is no name yet for the places he and his voice can go.' But despite (or because of) the accuracy of this observation, Buckley's commercial status diminished in direct proportion to his artistic achievements, and by the time of his ground-breaking masterpiece *Star-*

AND · HELLO

Tim Buckley, playing and wailing, in 1974. The strength and scope of Buckley's rock vocals were astonishing.

sailor (1971) the earlier public acclaim had dwindled to a hard core. *Starsailor* was an admirable work, an abstract and inspired fusion of avant-garde jazz and vocal experimentation, but it was a commercial disaster.

At a time when introspective singer-songwriters singing pretty, bland tunes reigned supreme, Buckley was just too inaccessible, too much of an original talent. However, Buckley and his partner Beckett refused to compromise their methods and began to branch out into other fields of creative writing, adapting novels for screenplays and scoring soundtracks for works like Joseph Conrad's *An Outcast Of The Islands*.

The singer recognised that his determination to develop an area of hitherto untouched territory was winning him no new friends. Embittered and depressed, he retired from the music business for a spell, teaching Ethnomusicology at California University and even working for a time as a chauffeur and gardener for Sly Stone.

In late 1972, however, he returned with his most overtly commercial effort, *Greetings From LA*. It was a sensual, soulful, sexual celebration, with a more accessible jazz-funk rhythmic foundation provided by a nucleus of Chuck Rainey (bass), Ed Greene (drums) and Joe Falsia (guitar). Buckley's voice was in as fine form as ever – particularly on 'Sweet Surrender', where his soaring wails, gasps and groans dripped sex – but he was now accused of selling out by the same people who had professed to being left cold by his jazzier excursions.

A fool's farewell

A not unsurprising lack of confidence bedevilled his final work for Frank Zappa's Discreet label. *Sefronia* (1974) represented a conscious, yet unconvincing return to the folkier sound of *Goodbye And Hello*. Buckley himself admitted that his come-back was 'calculated' and that his music was 'not as passionate as it used to be'. His private life, meanwhile, was at an all-time low after a divorce and a flirtation with hard drugs. On 29 July 1975, shortly after the release of the tellingly-titled and immensely disappointing *Look At The Fool*,

Tim Buckley died after ingesting a fatal dose of heroin and morphine.

While the artist's plea that he has been hard done by or ignored often indicates some kind of personal failing, in Buckley's case an informed reception from those who professed to have his best feelings at heart might have averted his slide into manic depression. Of his own technique, Buckley had said; 'An instrumentalist can be understood doing just about anything but people are geared to hearing something coming out of a mouth being words. I use my voice as an instrument.'

In retrospect, Tim Buckley has been granted the acclaim he deserved in his lifetime. He left behind a legacy of essential listening, but the posthumous praise is sadly too little and too late.   MAX BELL

Tim Buckley
Recommended Listening

Goodbye And Hello (Elektra K42070) (Includes: Once I Was, Morning Glory, Goodbye And Hello, No Man Can Find The War, Hallucinations, I Never Asked To Be Your Mountain); *Greetings From LA* (Warner Bros. WB 46176) (Includes: Move With Me, Get On Top, Sweet Surrender, Nighthawkin', Devil Eyes, Make It Right).

ALTHOUGH IT IS OFTEN SAID that Parsons single-handedly pioneered the country-rock style of the early Seventies, the sheer magnitude of this conceit tends to obscure his real contribution. For while Parsons had a natural feel for emotive phrasing, the right song to cover and the exact instrumental brew, he was unsure of these personal strengths. While he was a strong musical influence on the Byrds and, later, the Rolling Stones, his innate lack of confidence which drove him to become a heavy user of various drugs frequently prevented him from capitalising on a huge talent.

Parsons' early life lends weight to the contradictions that shaped his lifestyle. Born in Winterhaven, Florida, on 5 November 1946, he was brought up in Waycross, Georgia; his family were of Southern land-owning stock and immensely wealthy citrus fruit farmers. His given name was Cecil Ingram Connor, but he took the surname of his stepfather when his mother married again after his father's suicide in the late Fifties.

The young boy showed a taste for Elvis Presley and Buddy Holly, but was himself a real Southern gentleman, polite and well spoken. He was also the possessor of a substantial trust fund that would later finance his wilder exploits. His money allowed him to lead several bands, including a folk trio with Jim Croce and Kent Lavoie (later Lobo) and a band, the Shilohs, based in Greenville, South Carolina. Both played music that was traditional in content.

Gram Parsons was also studious at times; he attended Harvard, where he majored in theology and first formed a liking for the honest gospel and country material that he saw as an antidote to psychedelic rock; at the same time he was attracted to the ever-burgeoning West Coast fraternity of successful musicians.

White man's blues

At Harvard he formed the International Submarine Band, a group which specialised in a form of country that Parsons called his 'white soul music'. In particular he found the working-class connotations of country lyrics and their heady mixture of religious guilt and lust enormously appealing. The group recorded one album, *Safe At Home* (1968), including songs from established country artists such as Johnny Cash and Merle Haggard (Parsons' new idol) as well as bluesman Arthur Crudup's 'That's All Right'. Like Presley before him, Parsons saw a link between R&B, country and rock'n'roll. His ability to integrate the elements of all three provided the framework of a musical style, country-rock, for which he was to become justly famous.

On leaving Harvard and the International Submarine Band, Parsons happened to bump into the Byrds' Chris Hillman in a Los Angeles bank. At that time the Byrds had reached a hiatus, having said goodbye to both their folk-rock obsession and to David Crosby and Gene Clark. Hillman had a background in bluegrass and a mutual understanding was

GP

Gram Parsons: doomed genius of country rock

Above: The Parsons solo collection. GP *was the only one of these albums to be released in his lifetime.*

soon formed. Parsons joined the Byrds and heavily influenced the other members with his enthusiasm for new directions.

The resulting album, *Sweetheart Of The Rodeo* (1968), was one of those records whose reverberations took time to make themselves felt, yet to Parsons there was nothing new in the album's musical concepts, with gospel-flavoured country, such as the Louvin Brothers' 'The Christian Life', lying comfortably side by side with R&B, like William Bell's 'You Don't Miss Your Water', and electrified Dylan and Guthrie. Apart from Parsons' contributions (one of them, 'Hickory Wind' being an old International Submarine Band number) the album also included Merle Haggard's 'Life In Prison' and the traditional 'Blue Canadian Rockies'. What was different for the Byrds was the fashion in which they interpreted these songs, Parsons inspiring them to utilise pedal steel, banjo, mandolin and the guitar of Clarence White.

Parsons' sojourn with the Byrds was as brief as it was momentous. He refused to tour South Africa with them, due to his opposition to apartheid, and instead hitched up with the Rolling Stones, whom the Byrds had recently met on their UK tour.

Flying on the ground

On returning to Los Angeles, Parsons formed the Flying Burrito Brothers with bass-player Chris Ethridge, pedal-steel player Sneaky Pete Kleinow and Chris Hillman, who played rhythm guitar and mandolin.

The Burritos' first album, *The Gilded Palace Of Sin* (1969), was the first record to showcase Parsons' songwriting and singing. Among its many gems were numbers such as 'Hot Burrito #1' and 'Hot Burrito #2' (co-written with Chris Ethridge) and 'Wheels' and 'Sin City' (co-written with Chris Hillman). *The Gilded Palace Of Sin* brilliantly blended country with rock and R&B; Parsons' voice masterfully interpreted the record's tales of spiritual anguish and 'life in the fast lane', while the band (which initially included Popeye Phillips on drums) backed him to the hilt.

Despite the album's excellence, the public refused to pay attention to the band. Parsons became a frequent member of the Rolling Stones' entourage and even persuaded them to put the Burritos on the bill at Altamont. The Burritos' next album, *Burrito De Luxe* (1970) featured 'Wild Horses', a song especially written for the band by Mick Jagger and Keith Richards that was later to appear on the Stones' own *Sticky Fingers* (1971).

Shortly before the release of *Burrito De Luxe*, Parsons left the Burritos, his place being taken by singer-songwriter Rick Roberts. Parsons went on a two-year sabbatical, committing nothing to vinyl until 1973, by which time the country-rock style he had helped crystallise had become fashionable. He formed a group around three former members of Elvis Presley's backing band – ace guitarist James Burton, drummer Ron Tutt and pianist Glen D. Hardin.

Merle Haggard was lined up to produce the album but pulled out at the eleventh hour. Parsons thus decided to produce himself, enlisting the assistance of his old friend Rick Grech of Blind Faith and Traffic fame. Parsons had become both romantically and musically involved with the then virtually unknown singer Emmylou Harris, who consequently received second billing on the album cover. His increasingly croaky tenor blended superbly with Harris' impassioned soprano, most notably on 'We'll Sweep Out The Ashes In The Morning' and 'That's All It Took'.

Despite the excellence of Parsons' work, his personal life was anything but idyllic at this time. His affair with Harris resulted in acrimonious scenes with his wife, while a close friend, actor Brandon de Wilde, was found dead of a drug overdose.

Parsons' second solo album, *Grievous Angel* (1974), reflected these various pressures, indicating that the artist saw himself as born under a malicious star. Once more the album was inspired by notions of

Christian redemption and the overpowering temptations of lust and loose-living. In terms of production and content, however, it represented a considerable advance on *GP*; Gram's duetting with Emmylou reached new heights of tortured yearning on standards such as 'Hearts On Fire' and 'Love Hurts', while the haunting 'Brass Buttons' and the tragic '$1000 Wedding' must be numbered among his finest compositions. *Grievous Angel* was released posthumously in 1974 amid stories that Parsons' wife, jealous of her husband's relationship with Harris, had refused to

Below: Parsons seemed to imagine himself as a latterday Hank Williams, born under a bad sign. Here he relaxes with several beers.

allow the latter's picture to appear on the sleeve.

On 19 September 1973 Gram Parsons had been found dead in a motel near the Joshua Tree monument, a desert landmark that acted as a mystical spot for the singer and his friends. While the coroner said he died of natural causes, the people who discovered him knew that he had died of an overdose of morphine and alcohol. He was 26.

This was not the end of Gram Parsons' bizarre story, however. His body was kidnapped in most macabre circumstances at LA International Airport by two friends, one of whom, Phil Kaufman, claimed to have undertaken a cremation pact with Gram. Kaufman took the casket back to the Joshua Tree desert and set fire to it, as promised. He was soon apprehended, but was released when Parsons' family refused to press charges.

Parsons may have had his problems coping with everyday life, but as a communicator of sadness or rollicking good times he had few equals. When he sang, no matter how banal or tortured the lyric, you believed every word.   MAX BELL

Cooder's Story

Is Ry Cooder the archivist of American music?

THE CULT REPUTATION of American guitarist Ry Cooder was established early in his career. His 1970 debut album, *Ry Cooder*, set the style – obscure American blues, country and folk songs vigorously re-interpreted in a contemporary vein – while his subsequent three LPs included songs by Woody Guthrie, Huddie Ledbetter, Sleepy John Estes, Skip James and J. B. Lenoir along with interpretations of traditional material. During the 'progressive' era of the early Seventies, it seemed that Ry Cooder was singlehandedly attempting to remind America of its rich musical heritage.

This guitar for hire

Ryland Peter Cooder was born in Los Angeles on 15 March 1947. His father was an amateur guitarist with a large record collection that encompassed everything from Gilbert and Sullivan to Woody Guthrie. Cooder received his first guitar at the age of four, and his formative musical years were spent absorbing all manner of diverse musical styles, whether from records, the radio – where he particularly enjoyed the C&W stations broadcasting Johnny Cash, Hank Snow and Ernest Tubb – or at first hand, from blues legends like the Reverend Gary Davis, who helped shape Cooder's distinctive bottleneck guitar style.

Cooder landed a regular gig at an LA club, the Ash Grove, and the manager there suggested teaming him up with singer Jackie DeShannon, who was just beginning to make a name for herself as a songwriter. Cooder recalled that early duo as 'cock-eyed, but interesting'. Soon after, he joined the young Taj Mahal in a group, the Rising Sons. The band gigged around LA, recorded a single, 'Candy Man' and an LP (which was never released).

Cooder began working his way into the developing and remunerative LA session scene, despite the fact that he couldn't read music. By his own admission, it was 'all sorts of dumb stuff, Paul Revere and the Raiders, just another date in the can sort of thing'. But the experience was important in teaching Cooder about studio techniques and led to his forming a friendship with Jack Nitzsche, who helped Cooder land slightly more prestigious gigs. Cooder's masterly bottleneck playing was apparent on the first two Captain Beefheart and his Magic Band albums, although Cooder was never a full time member of the Magic Band, finding the Captain 'too weird'.

Nitzsche got Cooder involved on albums by Randy Newman, Phil Ochs, the soundtrack of *Candy* (1968), and – most importantly for Cooder's growing reputation – with the Rolling Stones. Cooder's mandolin was prominent on the Rolling Stones' version of Robert Johnson's 'Love In Vain' from their 1969 album, *Let It Bleed*. He

Above: Ry Cooder, in shades, with Sixties group the Rising Sons. Opposite: In the Eighties playing his Stratocaster guitar.

also contributed to the 1971 *Sticky Fingers*, with some flesh-crawling slide on 'Sister Morphine'. Cooder made distinctive contributions to the soundtrack of Nicolas Roeg's *Performance* (1970) – which starred Mick Jagger – and appeared along with the Stones and Nicky Hopkins on the *Jamming With Edward* album in 1972. But Cooder was never a regular member of the Stones camp, like, say, Gram Parsons.

Solo in the Seventies

By 1970, Cooder had landed a solo deal with the Reprise label, and his debut album was released that year. It elicited great critical praise, including favourable comments from Paul Simon, who cited Cooder's debut album as a great influence on his own solo initiation in 1972. From early on, Cooder's albums were quite distinctive, evincing a care and concern for the many strands which make up the fabric of American popular music. Initially branded as a musical archivist, Cooder's concern and enthusiasm for his music embraced folk, blues, R&B, cajun, Tex-Mex, rock'n'roll and jazz.

At the core, Cooder's own musical heritage was rich enough to assimilate all those influences, to produce music of a rich and rewarding nature. Over the years, Cooder has cited influences as diverse as Curtis Mayfield, the New Lost City Ramblers, the Swan Silvertones, Pop Staples and Hawaiian guitarist Joseph Spence, among others. A series of technically accomplished, evocative and emotive solo albums through the Seventies reflected these diverse musical strands and helped establish Cooder's reputation. While it took 1979's *Bop Till You Drop* to see Cooder breaking out of that cult rut,

each preceding album had separated a strand from the fabric and illuminated it.

Cooder's 1972 release, *Into The Purple Valley*, was a thematic album loosely based around the experiences of poor people during the Depression of the Thirties. It featured raunchy versions of folk and blues songs such as the traditional drifter's lament 'How Can You Keep On Moving', Leadbelly's 'On A Monday' and Woody Guthrie's chilling 'Vigilante Man'. Cooder continued his explorations of the American working man's experience with *Boomer's Story* released later that year.

The opening lines of the title cut – 'Come and gather all around me/Listen to my tale of woe' – set the tone for what remains Cooder's most introspective and in many ways most satisfying work. Among its many high-points were two beautiful guitar instrumentals which displayed Cooder's playing at its most sensitive and masterful, 'Dark End Of The Street' and 'Maria Elena'. The LP's songs included two particularly brooding blues redolent of death and despair by John Estes, 'President Kennedy' and 'Ax Sweet Mama', and a version of the American Civil War song 'Rally 'Round The Flag' that positively oozed weary cynicism.

The follow-up LP to the intensity of *Boomer's Story* was the upbeat *Paradise And Lunch* (1974), which saw him moving into a more polished, city-oriented, R&B/gospel sound that presaged such later good-time albums as *Bop Till You Drop* (1979) and *Borderline* (1980). The earnestness of Ry's singing on earlier recordings was replaced by an ironic, drawling delivery that was in perfect accord with the wit of numbers like 'Married Man's A Fool', 'Ditty Wa Ditty' and 'If Walls Could Talk'. The record also contained a rare Cooder composition, 'Tattler', a superbly executed cautionary tale about the problems of married life later covered by Linda

Ronstadt in 1976 on her *Hasten Down The Wind* album.

Cooder's choice of musicians was always impeccable, and he entered a particularly fruitful period with the brilliant accordionist Flaco Jiminez on two albums, *Chicken Skin Music* in 1976 and the live *Show Time* in 1977. Their version of the old Jim Reeves hit, 'He'll Have To Go' was a personal favourite of Cooder's.

Flogging a dead horse
The 1977 *Jazz* found Cooder wanting 'to provide a thread of alternative jazz settings to some great music that falls within the one hundred year scope of jazz in America.' It found him working with jazz greats like Earl Hines on songs by Bix Beiderbecke, Joseph Spence and Jelly Roll Morton. But Cooder acknowledged the album as a failure, and it remains the least favourite of his own recordings: 'Not much of a record, more an interesting experiment . . . To me it's a dead horse.'

However it was that album which turned film director Walter Hill onto Cooder's music and which led Cooder to compose the soundtrack for Hill's 1980 Western *The Long Riders*. Cooder's soundtrack credentials had been established earlier with *Performance* and Paul Schrader's *Blue Collar* (1978), but his later work included Walter Hill's *Southern Comfort* (1981), which had a cajun feel. Tony Richardson's *The Border* (1981) found Cooder back on the Tex-Mex border, working with Sam (the Sham) Samudio.

Top: Cooder steps out on stage in London. Above: Singer-songwriter John Hiatt, who began to work with Cooder in the Eighties.

By 1979, Cooder was tired of the 'musical custodian' tag, and his digitally-recorded *Bop Till You Drop* album finally brought him the belated commercial success he deserved. From the authoritative opening track, Leiber and Stoller's 'Little Sister', the album was a triumph. Vocally the album was superb, with Cooder utilising Chaka Khan and Bobby King. King was to

accompany Cooder on his 1980 and 1982 UK shows, along with Willie Green Jr.

The guitarist stuck with the R&B formula with his 1980 album *Borderline*, which marked the beginning of his association with singer-songwriter John Hiatt. The album drew on songs from the Fifties (the Cadillacs' 'Speedo Is Back'), the Sixties (Joe South's 'Down In The Boondocks'), and beyond. Crisp and assured as the album was, there was a feeling that Cooder was treading water, and this was compounded by his 1982 album, *The Slide Area*.

The Eighties saw Cooder concentrating on film work with soundtracks for *Paris, Texas, Alamo Bay* (both 1985), *Blue City* and *Crossroads* (both 1987). Also released in 1987, *Get Rhythm*—his first non-celluloid album for five years—saw him marking time in familiar R&B territory. "The Eighties are looking better for me," he had commented, "because people want to hear more of the sort of music I do." It seemed Cooder had carved his niche and was profiting accordingly.

PATRICK HUMPHRIES

INDEX

v

U.S. HIT SINGLES

1975

JANUARY

4 LUCY IN THE SKY WITH DIAMONDS *Elton John*
11 LUCY IN THE SKY WITH DIAMONDS *Elton John*
18 MANDY *Barry Manilow*
25 PLEASE MR POSTMAN *Carpenters*

FEBRUARY

1 LAUGHTER IN THE RAIN *Neil Sedaka*
8 FIRE *Ohio Players*
15 YOU'RE NO GOOD *Linda Ronstadt*
22 PICK UP THE PIECES *Average White Band*

MARCH

1 BEST OF MY LOVE *Eagles*
8 HAVE YOU NEVER BEEN MELLOW *Olivia Newton-John*
15 BLACK WATER *Doobie Brothers*
22 MY EYES ADORED YOU *Franki Valli*
29 LADY MARMALADE *Labelle*

APRIL

5 LOVIN' YOU *Minnie Ripperton*
12 PHILADELPHIA FREEDOM *Elton John*
19 PHILADELPHIA FREEDOM *Elton John*
26 ANOTHER SOMEBODY DONE SOMEBODY WRONG
   SONG *B J Thomas*

MAY

3 HE DON'T LOVE YOU (LIKE I LOVE YOU)
   Tony Orlando/Dawn
10 HE DON'T LOVE YOU (LIKE I LOVE YOU)
   Tony Orlando/Dawn
17 HE DON'T LOVE YOU (LIKE I LOVE YOU)
   Tony Orlando/Dawn
24 SHINING STAR *Earth Wind and Fire*
31 BEFORE THE NEXT TEARDROP FALLS *Freddie Fender*

JUNE

7 THANK GOD I'M A COUNTRY BOY *John Denver*
14 SISTER GOLDEN HAIR *America*
21 LOVE WILL KEEP US TOGETHER *Captain and Tennille*
28 LOVE WILL KEEP US TOGETHER *Captain and Tennille*

JULY

5 LOVE WILL KEEP US TOGETHER *Captain and Tennille*
12 LOVE WILL KEEP US TOGETHER *Captain and Tennille*
19 LISTEN TO WHAT THE MAN SAID *Wings*
26 THE HUSTLE *Van McCoy and the Soul City Symphony*

AUGUST

2 ONE OF THESE NIGHTS *Eagles*
9 JIVE TALKIN' *Bee Gees*
16 JIVE TALKIN' *Bee Gees*
23 FALLIN' IN LOVE *Hamilton, Joe Frank and Reynolds*
30 GET DOWN TONIGHT *KC and the Sunshine Band*

SEPTEMBER

6 RHINESTONE COWBOY *Glen Campbell*
13 RHINESTONE COWBOY *Glen Campbell*
20 FAME *David Bowie*
27 I'M SORRY *John Denver*

OCTOBER

4 FAME *David Bowie*
11 BAD BLOOD *Neil Sedaka*
18 BAD BLOOD *Neil Sedaka*
25 BAD BLOOD *Neil Sedaka*

NOVEMBER

1 ISLAND GIRL *Elton John*
8 ISLAND GIRL *Elton John*
15 ISLAND GIRL *Elton John*
22 THAT'S THE WAY I LIKE IT *KC and the Sunshine Band*
29 FLY ROBIN FLY *Silver Convention*

DECEMBER

6 FLY ROBIN FLY *Silver Convention*
13 FLY ROBIN FLY *Silver Convention*
20 THAT'S THE WAY I LIKE IT *KC and the Sunshine Band*
27 LET'S DO IT AGAIN *Staple Singers*

U.K. HIT SINGLES

1974

JANUARY

5 MERRY XMAS EVERYBODY *Slade*
12 MERRY XMAS EVERYBODY *Slade*
19 YOU WON'T FIND ANOTHER FOOL LIKE ME
   New Seekers
26 TIGER FEET *Mud*

FEBRUARY

2 TIGER FEET *Mud*
9 TIGER FEET *Mud*
16 TIGER FEET *Mud*
23 DEVIL GATE DRIVE *Suzi Quatro*

MARCH

2 DEVIL GATE DRIVE *Suzi Quatro*
9 JEALOUS FRIEND *Alvin Stardust*
16 BILLY DON'T BE A HERO *Paper Lace*
23 BILLY DON'T BE A HERO *Paper Lace*
30 BILLY DON'T BE A HERO *Paper Lace*

APRIL

6 SEASONS IN THE SUN *Terry Jacks*
13 SEASONS IN THE SUN *Terry Jacks*
20 SEASONS IN THE SUN *Terry Jacks*
27 SEASONS IN THE SUN *Terry Jacks*

MAY

4 WATERLOO *Abba*
11 WATERLOO *Abba*
18 SUGAR BABY LOVE *Rubettes*
25 SUGAR BABY LOVE *Rubettes*

JUNE

1 SUGAR BABY LOVE *Rubettes*
8 SUGAR BABY LOVE *Rubettes*
15 THE STREAK *Ray Stevens*
22 ALWAYS YOURS *Gary Glitter*
29 SHE *Charles Aznavour*

JULY

6 SHE *Charles Aznavour*
13 SHE *Charles Aznavour*
20 SHE *Charles Aznavour*
27 ROCK YOUR BABY *George McCrae*

AUGUST

3 ROCK YOUR BABY *George McCrae*
10 ROCK YOUR BABY *George McCrae*
17 WHEN WILL I SEE YOU AGAIN
   Three Degrees
24 WHEN WILL I SEE YOU AGAIN
   Three Degrees
31 LOVE ME FOR A REASON *Osmonds*

SEPTEMBER

7 LOVE ME FOR A REASON *Osmonds*
14 LOVE ME FOR A REASON *Osmonds*
21 KUNG FU FIGHTING *Carl Douglas*
28 KUNG FU FIGHTING *Carl Douglas*

OCTOBER

5 KUNG FU FIGHTING *Carl Douglas*
12 ANNIE'S SONG *John Denver*
19 SAD SWEET DREAMER *Sweet Sensation*
26 EVERYTHING I OWN *Ken Boothe*

NOVEMBER

2 EVERYTHING I OWN *Ken Boothe*
9 EVERYTHING I OWN *Ken Boothe*
16 GONNA MAKE YOU A STAR *David Essex*
23 GONNA MAKE YOU A STAR *David Essex*
30 GONNA MAKE YOU A STAR *David Essex*

DECEMBER

7 YOU'RE THE FIRST THE LAST MY
   EVERYTHING *Barry White*
14 YOU'RE THE FIRST THE LAST MY
   EVERYTHING *Barry White*
21 LONELY THIS CHRISTMAS *Mud*
28 LONELY THIS CHRISTMAS *Mud*

1975

JANUARY

4 LONELY THIS CHRISTMAS   *Mud*
11 LONELY THIS CHRISTMAS   *Mud*
18 DOWN DOWN   *Status Quo*
25 MS GRACE   *Tymes*

FEBRUARY

1 JANUARY   *Pilot*
8 JANUARY   *Pilot*
15 JANUARY   *Pilot*
22 MAKE ME SMILE   *Steve Harley/Cockney Rebel*

MARCH

1 MAKE ME SMILE   *Steve Harley/Cockney Rebel*
8 IF   *Telly Savalas*
15 IF   *Telly Savalas*
22 BYE BYE BABY   *Bay City Rollers*
29 BYE BYE BABY   *Bay City Rollers*

APRIL

5 BYE BYE BABY   *Bay City Rollers*
12 BYE BYE BABY   *Bay City Rollers*
19 BYE BYE BABY   *Bay City Rollers*
26 BYE BYE BABY   *Bay City Rollers*

MAY

3 OH BOY   *Mud*
10 OH BOY   *Mud*
17 STAND BY YOUR MAN   *Tammy Wynette*
24 STAND BY YOUR MAN   *Tammy Wynette*
31 STAND BY YOUR MAN   *Tammy Wynette*

JUNE

7 WHISPERING GRASS
    Windsor Davies and Don Estelle
14 WHISPERING GRASS
    Windsor Davies and Don Estelle
21 WHISPERING GRASS
    Windsor Davies and Don Estelle
28 I'M NOT IN LOVE   *10cc*

JULY

5 I'M NOT IN LOVE   *10cc*
12 TEARS ON MY PILLOW   *Johnny Cash*
19 GIVE A LITTLE LOVE   *Bay City Rollers*
26 GIVE A LITTLE LOVE   *Bay City Rollers*

AUGUST

2 GIVE A LITTLE LOVE   *Bay City Rollers*
9 BARBADOS   *Typically Tropical*
16 I CAN'T GIVE YOU ANYTHING (BUT MY LOVE)
    Stylistics
23 I CAN'T GIVE YOU ANYTHING (BUT MY LOVE)
    Stylistics
30 I CAN'T GIVE YOU ANYTHING (BUT MY LOVE)
    Stylistics

SEPTEMBER

6 SAILING   *Rod Stewart*
13 SAILING   *Rod Stewart*
20 SAILING   *Rod Stewart*
27 SAILING   *Rod Stewart*

OCTOBER

4 HOLD ME CLOSE   *David Essex*
11 HOLD ME CLOSE   *David Essex*
18 HOLD ME CLOSE   *David Essex*
25 I ONLY HAVE EYES FOR YOU   *Art Garfunkel*

NOVEMBER

1 I ONLY HAVE EYES FOR YOU   *Art Garfunkel*
8 SPACE ODDITY   *David Bowie*
15 SPACE ODDITY   *David Bowie*
22 D.I.V.O.R.C.E.   *Billy Connolly*
29 BOHEMIAN RHAPSODY   *Queen*

DECEMBER

6 BOHEMIAN RHAPSODY   *Queen*
13 BOHEMIAN RHAPSODY   *Queen*
20 BOHEMIAN RHAPSODY   *Queen*
27 BOHEMIAN RHAPSODY   *Queen*